NETWORKING THE FARM

For Diane

Networking the Farm

The social structure of cooperation and competition
in Iowa agriculture

RANDY ZIEGENHORN
University of Iowa

Routledge
Taylor & Francis Group

LONDON AND NEW YORK

First published 1999 by Ashgate Publishing

Reissued 2018 by Routledge
2 Park Square, Milton Park, Abingdon, Oxon, OX14 4RN
711 Third Avenue, New York, NY 10017, USA

Routledge is an imprint of the Taylor & Francis Group, an informa business

Publisher's Note
The publisher has gone to great lengths to ensure the quality of this reprint but points out that some imperfections in the original copies may be apparent.

Disclaimer
The publisher has made every effort to trace copyright holders and welcomes correspondence from those they have been unable to contact.

A Library of Congress record exists under LC control number: 98074702

ISBN 13: 978-1-138-32140-3 (hbk)
ISBN 13: 978-0-429-45254-3 (ebk)

Contents

List of Figures

List of Tables

1 Introduction

Many farmers in Iowa and other Midwestern states are joining swine production networks - cooperative endeavors to jointly produce and market pigs. In this work I present the results of an ethnographic study of twelve of these groups to evaluate their practical significance to farmers and their theoretical significance to our understanding of the social and economic organization of agricultural production. This study evaluates production networks among household producers in a market economy by providing an assessment of the current and potential role of network forms of organization. It also enhances our understanding of new forms of economic organization that don't fit the usual assumptions about the behavior of firms or households.

The key theoretical issue explored here is the role of networks of economic relations in the market economy. This study integrates theory from economic anthropology and the New Institutional Economics (NIE) to enhance the understanding of these networks. The NIE explains economic organization by reference to its institutional setting as well as by using models of individual motivation and choice. This can be seen as part of a broader structural analytic perspective that has emerged in a number of social sciences in recent years (see Wellman and Berkowitz 1988 for an overview). Although anthropologists made early contributions to structural analysis through the development of social network analysis (Barnes 1954, Boissevain 1974, Boissevain and Mitchell 1971, Bott 1971, Mitchell 1974), its core articulations have come from economists, economic sociologists, and organization theorists (Granovetter 1985, North 1981, Powell 1990). Anthropologists have recently reentered the debate over the structuralist perspective through their interest in the NIE (Acheson 1994, Douglas 1992, Ensminger 1992, Plattner 1984, 1989b). For anthropologists, the NIE not only has affinities with social network analysis but also parallels Barth's (1981) use of transaction as the key to understanding social process.

The NIE explains economic behavior in part by the use of standard neoclassical microeconomic assumptions about rational choice and individual decision making. One of the flaws of neoclassical theory is its inability to adequately explain the origins of firms as economic entities. In other words, why in a world of utility maximizing individuals do the transactions for some goods take place in the market while others take place within some larger hierarchical unit - particularly firms? Williamson (1975, 1985) described a continuum of transactional behavior from market based

1

to hierarchical (i.e. within the firm itself). By linking economic and non-economic phenomena this market-hierarchy continuum helps construct a framework for explaining both the origin of firms and the structure of an economy.

Although the NIE offers a more realistic view of firms than standard neoclassical economic theory, it still suffers from the limitations of its reliance on individual maximizing and rational decision making. It is in Wrong's (1961) terms still a particularly undersocialized account of economic behavior. A more useful approach may be taken by viewing markets and hierarchies as alternative forms of economic organization alongside a third form - networks. Networks as a form of economic organization are seen as constituted by a variety of reciprocal exchanges of goods and information between people. As such they are embedded in a series of negotiated relationships. The growing interest in analyzing the structure of the economy through networks of relationships has the potential to counter the undersocialized accounts of both neoclassical and the new institutional economics (Granovetter 1992, Burt 1992, Powell and Smith-Doerr 1994).

Recent anthropological approaches to the study of American agriculture have focused on the role of individual decision making to understand economic behavior (Barlett 1980, 1993, Gladwin and Truman 1989). The focus on decision making relies heavily on cognitive explanations for economic activity, an approach opposite but in many ways complementary to the structural point of view. The structural approach regards the pattern of relationships as the central focus in the study of economic systems. People still make choices, still decide, but the range of choices are contingent upon social and economic constraints and structures. Economic activities and organizations do not arise from the aggregate effects of individual choice but from the contingent effects of relationships. From this point of view, the analysis of market economies is best served by attempting to understand the process of economic transformation based on the overall structure of economic and social relationships (cf. Campbell, Hollingsworth, and Lindberg 1991, Friedmann 1988, Portz 1991, White 1988, Young 1991).

Economic changes that are rapidly transforming family farms are also transforming firms. As a result of these changes the analytic focus shifts from the attempt to delineate categories of economic actors (i.e. to define households and firms) to obtaining a holistic view of the pattern of relationships among all actors (Larson 1992, Jarillo 1988, Dore 1980). In that sense the unit of analysis is neither the household producer nor the capitalist firm but the industry which structures the activity of various economic actors (cf. Porter 1990).

The increasing industrialization of livestock production is transforming traditional household production in American agriculture into an agro-industrial system that is indistinguishable from other sectors of the industrial economy. This contrasts an exceptionalist perspective that sets agriculture apart from the industrial economy due to dynamics of the household labor force, retention of ownership over the means of production, or inherent ecological constraints. (cf. Chayanov 1966, Mann and Dickinson 1978, Bennett 1968, 1982). In response to changes in demographic, economic, and technological factors many farmers are forming joint ventures as well as entering into new arrangements with processors and input suppliers that call in to question the usefulness of continuing earlier attempts to analytically distinguish either family farms or agriculture itself from the industrial economy.

The structural approach to the study of economic organization presented here is particularly relevant to recent changes in swine production in Iowa. New networks of economic relations are emerging among farmers, corporate swine producers, packers, and lenders. This study describes these emerging relationships and assesses the theoretical value of a network-based approach to the study of economic organization.

The growth of swine producer networks is related to efforts by the land grant universities and pork producer organizations in Iowa and other states to promote new ways of organizing swine production. Most of these efforts appear to be in response to recent technological and economic changes. Changes in the understanding of swine health encourage the wide physical separation of animals at various stages of their growth cycle. However, such an approach is poorly suited to the typical Midwestern family farm, which integrates all phases of swine production on a single site, and in many cases under a single roof. While family farms have largely been unable to adopt this component system model, many corporations have adopted it relatively quickly. The result has been the rise of a number of large-scale vertically integrated firms that raise animals on widely dispersed sites. Many worry that the such firms will drive small producers out of business, both because of their alleged advantages in production efficiency as well as through their attempts to capture greater market share with packers.

The land grant universities and pork producer groups have responded to this threat by encouraging family farmers to join together in a variety of ways to compete with the large producers. These proposals include models of 'networks' for information sharing, joint production, and joint marketing. The model most commonly being proposed to farmers is the formation of a jointly owned corporation which moves parts of production off farms into facilities similar to those being built by the large producers. At the same time many farmers are responding to this advice with networking arrangements that are far different from those being proposed by land grant university experts. As a result, there is a significant gap between the kinds of networks proposed by the experts and the kinds of networks created by farmers and others who act upon these proposals.

This study was conducted in two phases. The first phase attempted to identify some of the salient internal relationships for understanding the organization of production networks. The second phase attempted to identify external relationships. One of the conclusions suggested by the initial study was that flexible, informal, and reciprocal exchanges among network members could provide a form of economic organization different from either traditional household production or the formation of hierarchical organizations. The second phase of this study looked at whether such relationships could occur between producer networks as well as among other players in the swine industry and what effect such relationships may have on competitive success.

The first phase of this study, funded by the Leopold Center for Sustainable Agriculture at Iowa State University, was carried out from January 1995 through July 1996. Two networks initially agreed to participate in this phase of the study. Fieldwork consisted of attending the business meetings of both groups as well as conducting semi-structured and structured interviews with the organizers and members of each group. Additional funding was received from the Leopold Center as well as the National Pork Producers Council to complete work on a handbook to aid farmers in establishing production networks. Preparation of the handbook added to the detailed focus on the two original groups by using rapid appraisal techniques on several groups (cf. Beebe 1995). The detailed focus provided an understanding of the day to day experiences of hog farmers that informed the kinds of questions asked in preparing the handbook. I maintained connections with the networks in the original study in order to evaluate their ongoing development.

In my original study of two networks I focused primarily on describing the conditions that could lead to the successful formation and long term maintenance of a network. The success of a network, in terms of its internal organization, hinges on the ability of the organizer to identify and link farms with compatible needs and characteristics. Such ability is directly tied to the organizer's structural position that allows access to vital information making possible the identification of compatible relationships among producers.

The role played by networks in the swine industry is the focus of the second phase of the study. Above I argued that networks may constitute another form of economic organization alongside household producers or firms. The second phase of this project was concerned with assessing the ability of networks to compete with other methods of organizing production, particularly large-scale corporate swine production. While the first phase of the study considered significant internal relationships among network participants, the second phase considered a crucial external relationship – the availability of credit. I repeatedly observed that once the internal specifications of a network arrangement could be agreed upon the members were often faced with the equally daunting challenge of obtaining financing. Much of the time spent in bringing a network into operation involves the production of detailed financial plans and negotiations with lenders. The ability to obtain credit is the chief barrier to entry or expansion in the swine industry today. This is an ethnographic observation that extends this study from the more parochial concerns of the organizational mechanics of networks to an assessment of their competitive position in the swine industry. In order to assess the ability of networks to obtain credit I compared the credit relationships of networks to those of other categories of producers by collecting the credit histories of four hundred farmers, networks, and corporate swine producers. I found, in the patterning of these relationships, a structural resemblance between the credit relationships in the industry and the internal organizational relationships of a network. Some of the largest corporate producers seem to have the same pattern of structural advantage in their credit relationships that network organizers have in the internal relationships of their networks. Understanding the role of these external 'credit networks' is as important to the eventual success of producer networks as the internal relationships involved.

In both the organizational study and the credit study I attempt to get at the patterning of relationships among the participants, from family farms to multinational corporations. Detecting these patterns is the key to the structural approach advocated here. Rather than trying to explain economic behavior in terms of static characteristics, choice, or material or technological determinism this approach seeks to discover the patterns that emerge in actual settings where economic activity occurs.

As opposed to the methodological individualism of neoclassical economics that posits people in either a purely competitive market or in a market-hierarchy continuum, this approach seeks to understand the emergence and maintenance of exchange relationships among individuals and between individuals and firms in the market economy. At the same time, as opposed to the view that sees individuals thoroughly embedded in a socially proscribed world, this study sees reciprocal relationships as an aspect of a distinctly 'economic' form of behavior in which it is sometimes possible to make choices. This is a highly contingent approach to economic behavior as opposed to those overly deterministic approaches that, in the elegance of their explanations, lose sight of people and the way they relate to each other.

Chapter 2 below introduces the theoretical issues addressed in this project. I explore the history of economic anthropology and the contributions to that field from the New Institutional Economics. I then review anthropological and sociological approaches to the study of industrial agriculture and tie the current state of these studies to concepts from the NIE.

Chapters 3 through 5 explore the characteristics of producer networks. Chapter 3 provides an in depth case study of two networks. Chapter 4 looks at other networks in order to highlight some of the themes brought out in chapter 3. Chapter 5 presents a model for cooperation that explains the internal organization of producer networks.

Chapter 6 provides an overview of networking and the broad range of groups who have taken an interest in promoting this new production strategy. Chapter 6 also provides background information on the swine industry in Iowa, particularly the rise of large-scale production by corporations.

Chapter 7 presents the results of the credit study and suggests a model for competition. Finally, in chapter 8, I draw conclusions about both the cooperative and competitive models that tie in to the theoretical issues raised at the beginning of the work.

2 Economies and Farmers: An Overview

The Development of Theory in Economic Anthropology: The Role of the New Institutional Economics

This section concerns the study of economic behavior and institutions by anthropologists. It discusses what sort of knowledge we hope to gain about economies, what the object of that study should be, and what constitutes convincing explanation. Although I am primarily concerned with how these questions are answered by anthropologists, many of the ideas discussed come from economists, political scientists, economic historians, and sociologists. Below I discuss the prospects for generalization in economic anthropology arguing that anthropological generalizations are more likely to be constructed as models rather than formal scientific theories. I also review the history of theoretical debates in anthropology from Malinowski to the present and suggest ways in which the New Institutional Economics (NIE) can address some of the unresolved dilemmas confronting both economists and anthropologists. Finally, I suggest ways in which the insights of anthropologists may contribute to the advancement of the NIE. The overall argument of this chapter is that it is impossible to construct adequate explanations of the development of economies (or to define the 'economic') without constructing a theory of individual behavior as well as one of institutions. Economic theories based solely on the behavior of individuals assume away the problem of social order - the role of organizations, social structure, power, and ideology in economic life. At the same time those theories which are based solely on institutions assume away the problem of human choice - the role of preferences, incentives, and the decisions of individuals in economic life. In effect one sort of explanation does away with the observed complexity inherent in human affairs while the other does away with the deductive and parsimonious value of a focus on the individual. While one position or the other has dominated economic anthropology in certain periods the possibility now exists for a synthesis of both individualistic and institutional forms of economic explanation.

7

These theoretical issues provide a backdrop for the ethnographic material in subsequent chapters. As I observed farmers negotiating with one another I became aware of the subtle tension between the choices available to the individual, his or her knowledge of those choices, and the structure of the system which determines what the choices will be. To attempt to force my observations into one or another of the theoretical frameworks that have been used to explain economic behavior, would do an injustice to the complexity of the events I witnessed. Instead I attempt to synthesize the approaches of anthropologists and economists, approaches that have been brought closer together by the New Institutional Economics. In the end such an approach remains primarily 'anthropological' inasmuch as it attempts both to modify theory on the basis of ethnographic evidence and to apply that modified theory to further aid in understanding the particular events.

Economists, starting with a radically simplified set of assumptions about individual decision making, have developed a complex and increasingly formal set of deductive propositions to explain economic behavior. Defenders of economics point to the considerable success of microeconomic theory in coordinating behavior in market economies and point out that economics is often a normative, not a positive, science (e.g. Friedman 1953). In short, it aims not at explanation but at prescription. The prescription for non-market economies has been to shed themselves of a host of externalities that constrain the optimization of their economic performance. Anthropologists have largely insisted that the understanding of economic matters had to proceed from the empirical study of actual behavior (Plattner 1989a). Generalizations if they could be made at all were made inductively. The result of attention to actual behavior was to show the inaccuracies of the universal assumptions and prescriptive aims of economists. Sociologists and anthropologists have frequently argued that economic science is a reflection of capitalism in state societies and that cross-cultural studies largely disproved the universality of economic laws. At the same time that they were slaying the dragon of economics, anthropologists discovered the enemy within: broad disagreement over their ability to generate inductive generalizations about economies that applied cross culturally. If the road to hell for economists was paved with the increasing mathematical formality of their theories, the same road for anthropologists was paved with the anti-generalizing sentiment of historical and hermeneutic approaches to ethnographic evidence. In the former case each time and place are unique and valid generalization is unlikely, in the later each observer is unique and each interpretation equally (in)valid (Ortner 1984, Marcus and Fisher 1986, Spiro 1992:3-53).

In recent years, a number of economists and anthropologists, as well as political scientists and sociologists, have started to ask if some common ground can be found between their disciplines. The impetus behind much of the recent cross-fertilization between these disciplines is an attempt to reconcile the disparate claims of deductive and inductive statements about economies. Economists, especially economic historians, working within the NIE framework have shown a willingness to modify the assumptions of neoclassical economic theory with more empirical evidence (see Eggertsson 1990:3-79 for a review). At the same time some anthropologists have shown an interest in not only aspects of neoclassical economics but in projects in anthropology that apparently went out of fashion some 30 years ago in favor of the interpretive approach (Acheson 1994:29, Ensminger 1992:16). As Plattner has noted there is a need in anthropology for both historical particularistic work and for work of a more social scientific or generalizing nature (1989a:13).

Barth (1981) noted that anthropologists often construct eclectic models as a means of dealing with the variety of facts with which they are confronted. Such attempts at model building are often discarded once contradictory evidence is uncovered. Barth's goal was the construction of 'generative' models - such models would, through logical operations, generate forms which could be subject to empirical verification. These generative models are not homologous with empirical conditions, that is, they are not arrived at inductively but by abstracting certain key elements from social life and performing logical (i.e. deductive) operations on them. Although his view of economics is based on fundamentally different assumptions than those of Barth, Godelier proposes a similar relationship between formal economic models and empirical observation (1972:262-3). For Godelier formal models help present 'a series of questions to be put to the facts' (ibid.) For Barth and Godelier the importance of the model is to provide a stronger generalization than can be derived from induction alone.

The varying emphases given to induction and deduction has also occasioned much debate between anthropologists and economists. The exchange between Herskovits and Knight reproduced in the second edition of Herskovits's *Economic Anthropology* is representative of this debate (Herskovits 1952). Knight, reacting to Herskovits's claim that anthropology could provide empirical tests of economic theory, takes the position that deductive theory is fundamentally independent of empirical verification.

Knight argued that attempts to criticize economics for the failure of certain of its principles to conform to observation merely mistook the respective roles of deduction and induction in science (Herskovits 1952:512).

The question of the origin of economic phenomena is the key to both neoclassical economics and Durkheimian sociology. For the former analysis begins with the individual (Smelser and Swedburg 1994:5). The analysis of demand begins with the theory of utility, the starting point of which is the ability of individuals to define and order their preferences (Samuelson and Nordhaus 1992:83). In contrast, Durkheim argues that the individual is not the analytic starting point for either the economy or society. In *The Division of Labor in Society* he argues that the flaw of 19th century political economy lay in its emphasis on utility (1949:233). The result of using this individualistic desire for happiness as the basis for analysis is psychological reductionism (1982:40). The problem with the assumed place of the individual by 19th century utilitarians and economists is that society is deduced from individual behavior (1949:279). For Durkheim, rather, 'individuals are much more a product of common life than a determinant of it' (1949:338).

Early influential works by European anthropologists helped set the tone of the debate over the value of western economics for the study of 'primitive' societies. The authors rejected the individual as the starting point for the analysis of 'primitive' economies and insisted that economies are intimately linked to social and religious life (Malinowski 1984, Mauss 1990, Thurnwald 1965). By the late 1930s, however, the situation had changed and influential works in economic anthropology appeared which attempted to realign the discipline with neoclassical economics (Firth 1939, Goodfellow 1939, Herskovits 1952). Again, issues concerning the centrality of the individual and the place of the economy in society fed the controversy.

In contrast with the accommodation to economic assumptions Polanyi argued that western economics was based on a fundamentally flawed conception of human behavior: that individual interest drove economic life (Polanyi 1944). Like Malinowski, Polanyi argued that 'man's economy, as a rule, is submerged in his social relationships' (1944:46). This submerged economy, which he later termed 'embedded', is characterized not by the individual calculus of gain, but by the socially derived economic principles of reciprocity, redistribution, and householding. These forms characterized all economic life prior to the emergence of capitalism.

In tracing the emergence of capitalism, Polanyi demonstrated that the idea of a self-regulating market 'demands nothing less than the institutional separation of society into an economic and political sphere' (1944:71). Polanyi sought to establish the proposition that 'outside of a system of price making markets economic analysis loses most of its relevance as a method of inquiry into the working of the economy' (1957:247). The history of capitalism illustrated the degree to which free market liberalism was imposed on the preexisting economic organization. Capitalism and its justification in economic science was a revolutionary undertaking. The key to understanding economies came from distinguishing between the substantive and formal definitions of economic - 'the substantive meaning of economic derives from man's dependence for his living upon nature and his fellows' (1957:243). The formal meaning, as noted above, derives from the analysis of situations involving choice and 'the logic of rational action' (ibid.).

The formalist/substantivist debate in anthropology followed on the heels of Polanyi's work and elaborated on the positions taken by various anthropologists up to that time (major positions in this debate are found in Leclair and Schneider 1968; Dalton 1967, 1969; Schneider 1974; Sahlins 1972). Posner (1980) described the controversy as a sterile debate characterized by misunderstandings of economic theory on both sides. At the same time he credited both sides with making positive contributions to the understanding of primitive economics from both the rational maximizing standpoint and the role of institutions in primitive economic life. What seems clear from the debate among anthropologists over the relevance of neoclassical economic theory is the usefulness of ceding some ground to both formalist and substantivist principles - to methodological individualism and to embeddedness in institutions - as useful heuristics in understanding some aspects of economies. This is, in effect, the conclusion reached by Cancian (1966). He argued that the two points of view are noncontradictory. What Cancian's solution leaves unanswered is how to specify the link between individual behavior and institutions. What is missing is any causal connection between choice as *a priori* theory and institutions as *a posteriori* constraints.

Among economists Coase is the earliest proponent of what came to be known as the new institutional economics. He opened the door to more realistic analyses of the economy by introducing the concept of transaction cost. Coase (1937) argued that the existence of firms could not be accounted for by neoclassical economic theory. Under the neoclassical assumptions of perfect information, ordered preferences and cost free transacting there is no reason that any transactions for goods should take place outside of the market itself - in short neoclassical economic theory suffers from the embarrassment of providing no explanation for the organization of production within firms. Coase's key observation was that transacting in the market is not only risky but also costly. These 'transaction costs' include the costs of discovering who the relevant players in a particular market are, what level of prices exist, the costs of negotiating and measuring transactions, and the costs of enforcing agreements. The higher the cost of carrying out transactions in the market, the greater the likelihood that the entrepreneur will seek to acquire similar goods and services through the hierarchic organization of a firm - i.e. through directing the work of others rather than bargaining in the market - if that can result in an overall lowering of transaction costs. Coase argued that if this idea were to have value for economists it must meet two tests - it must be both logical and real. Coase's call for empirical confirmation of economic theory echoes the objections to neoclassical economics from his contemporaries in sociology and anthropology. At the same time the addition of an elegant assumption of costly transacting didn't preclude the fundamental starting point of economic analysis in the choices made by individuals.

Through the work of North, Coase's insights about transaction costs have taken on substantial importance for economic theory (North 1981, 1990). In North's view transacting is made costly due to the specific institutional form in which that transacting takes place. Institutions are the 'rules of the game', the human regulations governing behavior and affecting the availability of information. The response of individuals to such institutional constraints is to cooperate with others to modify the institutions. The process of that modification, carried out in various organizational forms, from farms to workshops to factories, stretches the theorizing of neoclassical economics to embrace the actual historical development of institutions as a key element in explaining the relative performance of economies.

The new institutional economics uses the concept of transaction cost to develop a theory of institutions based on individual decision making. Unlike earlier neoclassical theories, the NIE modifies the unrealistic assumptions about perfect information and rational actors. NIE theorists see rationality as bounded and individuals as cooperating in arrangements that earlier theorists dismissed as market failure. The 'friction' that characterizes exchange in the real world provides the stimulus for institution building.

The starting point in rational choice theory is retained but NIE theory sees the individualistic basis more as a base line or a statistical null hypothesis against which to compare actual outcomes (Rawski 1996:5).

The analysis of transaction costs allows the application of a choice theoretic perspective to a number of earlier approaches taken by anthropologists. Posner and Landa have examined the kula (studied earlier by Malinowski) as an institutional means of reducing transaction costs thus facilitating trade through the establishment of trust (Posner 1980:25, Landa 1994:141-172, Malinowski 1984). North applies the transaction costs framework to Polanyi's concept of the appropriational movements of goods. Just as the costs of locational movements - production, transformation, and transportation - affect exchange, so too do the costs of appropriational movements - negotiating, measuring and enforcing agreements (North 1977). Similarly, Geertz's analysis of the role of clientelization as a means of counteracting high information costs in a Moroccan bazaar can be seen as an example of minimizing transaction costs (Geertz 1992, Posner 1980).

Ensminger argues that Barth provides the most compatible foundation for applying the concepts of the NIE to anthropology (Ensminger 1992:8-12, Barth 1981). Barth argues that individual choices and their aggregate emergent social patterns, while distinguishable, cannot be analytically separated. Economists typically limit the range of their explanations by limiting the number of factors considered endogenous to the system. The problem for anthropologists is 'where to locate endogenous sources of change in a system' (Barth 1981:80). Ensminger advocates Barth's concept of the stepwise model as a solution to the problem - a kind of shifting back and forth between the individual and institutions. The importance of such a model is that it incorporates some specification of the link between individual choice and institutional context. Ensminger frames the importance of this issue in a way that could be applied to the substantivist position when she notes, 'It is one thing to say institutions matter; it is another to explain how they matter'(1992:17).

The detailing of the influence of particular cultures - those broadest of institutions - on constructing what is estimable in the minds of their members may be one of the key anthropological contributions to the NIE. As Douglas has noted 'standards of what counts as estimable vary' (Douglas 1992:192). Cost is not the same to the Filipino fisher as it is to the Islamic money lender or to the Iowa farmer. What makes the synthesis of anthropological and NIE theory useful is the lessening of the dichotomy between methodological individualism and social embeddedness. The two approaches provide a rationale for studying choice under institutional constraints that constitutes a significant advance over their earlier adamant opposition.

Bates (1989, 1995) critiques the NIE by placing greater emphasis on the role of states in exercising power and determining the kinds of (or lack of) available institutions. Bates echoes concerns familiar to anthropologists and Marxists - the differentials of power that are often obscured by rational choice theories (1995:42):

> The image conveyed in the new institutionalism is that of economic actors, frustrated in their efforts to transact in markets, structuring non-market institutions that will enable them to transcend their dilemma and thereby attain welfare enhancing outcomes. The reality is that non-market institutions are often created in the legislature or court room or by economic actors who anticipate the appeal of others within such political arenas. Property rights, contract law, the power to regulate the production and exchange of commodities - these and other economic institutions are created by the state.

For Bates the solution lies in addressing politics and the state which have been downplayed by the NIE. Solutions to economic problems depend, in Bates's view, on more than the cost of transacting - they depend on the structure of politics (1995:45). In many cases the costs of transacting are allocated by the state. Bates' work on the transition to market economies in Kenya attempts to introduce the concepts of power and ideology, central to Marxist analyses, to the relatively politics-free NIE theory (Bates 1989). Bates's critique of Scott (1976) is similarly based on Bates's objection that individual actions do not produce collective outcomes by a simple process of aggregation (Bates 1990).

Economic anthropology attempts to generalize by constructing models of the economic behavior of individuals and organizations in the context of their historical embeddedness in institutions. The economy is inextricably tied to the institutional intersection of choice and constraint over the production and distribution of goods and services. In light of its holistic outlook anthropology contributes to the study of economies by including as endogenous to the working of an economy much that economists have treated as exogenous. Inasmuch as this work begins *in medias res*, it is uncommitted to any particular emphasis on one causal factor or the other (individuals or institutions), but looks for instances of models that offer a range of possible causes and outcomes. The value of a model lies not so much in its ability to predict specific sequences of events but to account for those events which do occur in light of the logical consequences of the model. The value of a model lies in its comparative usefulness, its ability to account for a wide range of phenomena. As Barth noted, models foster both the 'naturalist's stance of 'watching and wondering'' and the use of 'comparative analysis as the methodological equivalent of experiment' (1981:9,33). The new institutional economics has added a dimension to neoclassical economics that ties it to the empirical insights of anthropologists. In light of the connection to institutional theory, the long running controversy between anthropologists and economists is lessened. While 'institutions' and 'culture' may be different ways of expressing the same thing, it is the connection between individual choices and institutions or cultures through the costliness of transacting that offers to reconcile the two approaches. The task for the anthropologist and the new institutional economist alike is to articulate in precise detail the practical working out (or lack thereof) of the assumptions and possibilities of this theory in the broadest possible range of times and places.

Anthropological and Sociological Approaches to the Study of Industrial Agriculture in the U.S.

In the previous section I argued that the New Institutional Economics (NIE) provides a framework that complements anthropological approaches to the study of economies. The NIE's focus on the institutional setting and that setting's influence on individual decision making embraces two perspectives that have frequently divided both anthropologists and economists. In this section I review the work of anthropologists and rural sociologists studying industrial agriculture in the United States. The literature discussed is theoretically and methodologically diverse and at first glance might appear to be concerned only tangentially with issues related to the NIE. I argue instead that the questions posed, the empirical evidence presented, and the issues surrounding the research can be brought into sharper focus from the perspective of the NIE.

Industrial agriculture is used here broadly as the term to identify the agricultural system that prevails in the United States and Western European countries and that increasingly dominates developing nations as well. In its simplest sense an 'industrial' agriculture is defined by the increasing use of fossil fuel based inputs and the products of factories in agricultural production - fertilizers, pesticides, complex machines (Barlett 1989). It is opposed to various traditional agricultural systems which rely to a greater extent on the production of needed inputs at the household or village level, often through biological processes rather than more complex technologies. Attendant with the increasing use of the manufactured inputs is the rise of the widely noted technology treadmill. Productivity increases associated with new technologies create economic shifts (commodity gluts, price changes) that commit producers to a process of continuous change and the adoption of ever more expensive yet productive innovations (Cochrane 1993, Barlett *op.cit.*). Additionally, industrial agriculture displaces large numbers of workers.

However, the focus of a definition of industrial agriculture on its strictly technological aspects ignores the institutional context in which such changes are carried out. More than a simple calculus of gain on the part of farmers influences the introduction and adoption of new production strategies. Control over such technologies is frequently held by a few large private firms. The property rights of these firms, their ability to maintain ownership of both the physical technologies as well as the intellectual properties that sustain such technologies, is underwritten by states. To understand the complex nature of agricultural industrialization requires more than an assessment of technological change. A focus on technology ignores the wider institutional setting (the particular convergence of private interests and the interests of states in the food production systems) which interacts to shape the technological, economic and social aspects of industrial agriculture. Thus, too strictly locating the definition of 'industrial' agriculture in technology masks not only the enormous economic and social pressures on populations adopting these new technologies but also the very origin of such systems in the efforts of states to write the rules of the game in society.

Below I discuss these issues in light of two pioneering ethnographic works on American agriculture – Miner's *Culture and Agriculture* (1949) and Goldschmidt's *As You Sow* (1978). I then look at the revival of interest in Goldschmidt's study by rural sociologists and the considerable literature generated by that discussion.

In 1939 Horace Miner was hired by the USDA's Bureau of Agricultural Economics to conduct a cultural study of a Midwestern farming community. With his family, Miner took up residence in Iowa

Falls, Iowa with the goal of conducting an ethnographic field study of surrounding Hardin County. Miner's work was intended to be part of a larger project aimed at producing ethnographic portraits of rural communities across the US. The project is interesting for two reasons - 1) Miner's conclusions about the effects of agricultural industrialization and government intervention on rural life; and 2) his work was censured by the Agriculture Department and, published years later, remains almost unknown today.

That the study was carried out ethnographically is interesting in that the 1940s marked the end of one predominant school of investigation in rural sociology and the beginning of another. Miner's study came on the heels of nearly a half-century of community studies conducted by rural sociologists at land grant universities. Buttel *et al.* (1990) describe the use of research teams and appraisal methods resembling current rapid appraisal techniques in anthropology. Although many of these projects eventually led away from fine-grained ethnography in favor of broad social surveys, the attempt to build holistic studies of rural community life was well established in rural sociology by the 1940s. The rural sociology of the 1950s through the 1970s was, by contrast, characterized by concerns with behavioral and social psychological measures relating to the diffusion and adoption of innovations, the values of farmers, and the relationship between education and achievement among farm families (Buttel *et al.* 1990:43-72).

In Hardin County, Miner found many of the conditions that Walter Goldschmidt would describe in greater detail in *As You Sow*, particularly, the increasing urbanization of rural life (Goldschmidt 1978). Miner noted the decrease in interdependence among farmers despite a long history of family and community cooperation. He also noted the growing production ethic of farming coupled with a reticence on the part of farmers to keep accurate accounts of income and expenses (1949:66). The household economies that Miner described were devoted more to increasing the scope of the farm operation as a means of surviving and competing for new technologies than as a business investment (Miner 1949:60-74).

Miner also noted the increasing disappearance of rural neighborhoods - 'with respect to social action groups all those larger than the farm are politically defined' - and the dependence of the farm on those larger political units (1949:38). This relation of the farm to the city was, in Miner's view, responsible for the shift from a distinctively rural outlook or ideology to one based on the values of urban communities. Miner also noted the disintegrating economies of many small towns as the newly mobile rural residents traveled to larger commercial centers.

The portions of Miner's ethnography which apparently drew the wrath of the USDA and caused the work to be dropped from the Rural Life Studies Series were Miner's observations about the newly instituted USDA programs under the Agricultural Adjustment Act of 1936. Miner contrasts the production ethic of the farmers with the government established incentives to curtail production. At the heart of the issue is what he describes as a gap between the rural culture and the social programs of the New Deal. Miner saw the acceptance of cash payments to reduce production as an affront to the farmers' traditional emphasis on production. At the same time the concept that the market itself was flawed, that government payments represented a 'parity' level between the cost of producing a crop and its going market price, apparently made little headway with farmers. Miner notes that farmers overwhelmingly accepted cash payment from the government neither as relief nor as the expression of economic retribution but as payment for a service provided.

Miner's short work is remarkable for detecting many of the key issues not only in the development of industrial agriculture but in the relationship between social scientists and the agricultural community. In his introduction Miner notes that 'the attempt to make a community study bear upon the implications of a controversial national governmental policy was a tactical error' (1949:iii). His implication is that the USDA's purpose in commissioning the study was not to enter into a political debate but to produce relatively benign 'portraits' of rural life. Despite the tactical error the strategic accomplishment of Miner's work is substantial. As rural sociology turned inward to study the mental gymnastics of adoption and diffusion, Miner's work points out the enduring importance of using ethnography to uncover issues that are at the heart of economic change - local cultural values and the coordinated efforts on the part of industry and the state to direct change that often conflicts with those values. In that clash, and in the competition for resources that followed, lies the institutional crucible of modern industrial agriculture.

In contrast to Miner's short work, Goldschmidt's massive *As You Sow* explores many of the same issues but in far greater detail (Goldschmidt 1978). Goldschmidt produced two studies of California farming communities in the late 1940s documenting the changes associated with the industrialization of the surrounding agricultural economy. Goldschmidt argued that the rise of large scale industrial agriculture in California brought about the urbanization of rural life and an overall decline in living standards in nearby towns. In communities where smaller farms were prevalent 'the institution of small independent farmers is indeed the agent which creates the homogeneous community, both socially and economically democratic' (1978:281). In addition to studying the effects of agricultural industrialization on rural life much of Goldschmidt's study is oriented toward the study of labor and class relations.

Goldschmidt focused on the material conditions underlying economic life but also recognized the primary importance of understanding the role of social organization in industrial agriculture. His ethnography also reveals the importance of mental representations or models of reality for economic life. In one case he describes the sense of identity held by farm workers that prevents them from fully understanding their own position (Goldschmidt 1978:232):

> their occupation history shows that a large proportion of them have been farmers in the past. They do not identify themselves with a laboring class because they are only temporarily non-farmers, and certainly only temporarily farm laborers. At least that is the way most of them feel. and it is certainly the way in which they want to be identified to the community in which they live. where they readily recognize that labor status means no social status.

Elsewhere, describing the creation of a class system in the rapidly industrializing rural areas, Goldschmidt asks a key question for researchers trying to understand the cultural and institutional basis of an economic system, 'how does the dominant group control the submissive and what are the checks against this control in the hands of the latter' (1978:148).

In a final chapter added to the 1978 reprint of *As You Sow*, Goldschmidt detailed the attempts on the part of agribusiness interests, large farmers, and politicians to discredit and suppress his study. What primarily provoked this hostility was the direct challenge Goldschmidt's study presented to the attempts of agribusiness interests to set aside restrictions on the size of landholdings in California's irrigated agricultural districts. By suggesting that some principle of equity ought to guide agricultural policy Goldschmidt articulated an entirely different set of future possibilities for California than those seen by agribusiness elites (1978:257):

> Our discussion of equity revolves around two fundamental questions: (1) equity for whom and (2) equity in what. For it is necessary to see who fails in getting his share in the values of rural life and what these values are which are not fairly apportioned.

Goldschmidt's lasting contribution was to document the ways in which the organization and structure of industrial agriculture impacts the social, cultural, and economic lives of those living in rural communities. The censure which these conclusions generated indicated a concerted effort on the part of government and industry to embrace the industrial agricultural model. Both the Goldschmidt and Miner studies and the reactions to them form a baseline for the sociological and anthropological study of industrial agriculture in post war America. Research on one of the key institutions of society, its food production system, came to be intensely tied to the political and economic institutions of that society - a structure which attempts to direct the benefits of the system.

If the venture into US agriculture by anthropologists was short lived at least it had an impact. Miner and Goldschmidt both produced studies based on ground level ethnographic work that called into question the rapid industrialization of US agriculture that took place during and after the Second World War. In Goldschmidt's case, that study would form the basis for a lengthy debate among a later generation of rural sociologists. In the nearer term, however, most anthropologists attended to their traditional focus on non-Western cultures and work abroad.

The analysis of American agriculture was left to rural sociologists who were busy providing the data for one of the largest social engineering projects ever attempted - the wholesale transfer of food production from household based production units which employed over a third of the US workforce to concentrated industrial enterprises owned and worked by a few. This model of development, exported around the world by the US government, businesses, and scientists, would, it was argued, 'free' unproductive agricultural labor for more productive work in factories while increasing the efficiency of farming operations (Cochrane 1993:235-257).

Much of the history of post war anthropology has to do with the study of these changes as they were exported to various traditional agricultural societies around the world. At the same time, anthropologists paid little attention to these changes occurring in the US. In retrospect, both of these works are prophetic in their vision of the effects of agricultural industrialization and the politicization of research into the consequences of those effects. Both provide a valuable starting point from which to view the institutional setting of agriculture in America.

The setting of rural sociology was the subject of Friedland's 1982 review of the discipline in which, citing Goldschmidt's experience, he argued (1982:596-7):

> 'rural sociology is not a 'free' subdiscipline; rather it should be characterized as 'bureaucratic' or 'tied'...

> ...because agricultural sciences are 'tied' they experience significant internal tensions between orientations toward professionalism and to disciplinary association, on the one hand, and productionism and justification of public support on the other.'

In effect, rural sociology was captive to its setting in the land grant universities (cf. Hightower 1978).

Friedland captures two key points to emerge from the work of Goldschmidt and Miner - 1) analyses of industrial agriculture that challenge the social consequences of this industrialization threaten both private interests and the state (and the often blurry middle ground between the two) and 2) at the same time studies that seek to tailor themselves not to arouse the ire of these powerful interests may become irrelevant.

By the early 1970s rural sociologists began to produce a number of studies that directly questioned the social consequences of agricultural industrialization. Heffernan (1972) studied the degree of alienation from the surrounding community experienced by workers on a large-scale poultry farm. Hefernan's study is notable for his use of a field study in the midst of the rural sociological obsession with statistics and theoretical abstractions. On the basis of structured interviews with workers he concluded that the workers in the corporate farm setting were much less involved in community life than family farmers. Corporate managers were, on the other hand, much more involved in the same community activities than the family farmers. This emphasis on the extremes in community involvement that resulted from the corporate farms led Heffernan to conclude that industrial farming was bringing about a class structure 'which undermines the traditional American ideal of equality'(1972:497). Heffernan also suggested at least some consistency between the Marxian and Jeffersonian outlooks on the ownership of the means of production and the relation of ownership to participation in social and political life (1972:484; cf. Heffernan and Lasley 1978).

Although Heffernan did not cite Goldschmidt's earlier study his work takes a similar approach by questioning the consequences or agricultural restructuring for local communities. Two years later Rodefeld (1974) reintroduced Goldschmidt's work and helped launch a 20 year cottage industry among rural sociologists testing the 'Goldschmidt hypothesis' by looking at the relationship between various measures of structural change in agriculture and the quality of rural life. The term 'Goldschmidt hypothesis' is something of a misnomer given that Goldschmidt didn't really pose a hypothesis nor did he even get a chance to complete a second round of research (due to a loss of funding because of the controversy he provoked) that would have helped validate his original findings. Additionally, Goldschmidt's findings came from the careful ethnographic examination of life in two communities.

The subsequent development and testing of the Goldschmidt hypothesis by rural sociologists relies not on ethnography but on statistical studies based on the U.S. Census of Agriculture. Four important drawbacks characterize the Goldschmidt hypothesis literature: first, the breadth of statistical data and its remove from real life forgoes the descriptive power of ethnography and the ability to detect phenomena in a local context; second, the reliance on 'official' data limits the analysis to those categories deemed worth collecting by Census officials in the first place, introducing the possibility of politically motivated constraints on the collection of the primary data; third, in the end the analysis of this data remains primarily correlational - causation can only be suggested, while differentials in wealth and power as well as particular local circumstances influencing structural change are ignored; fourth, the debate became mired down over the taxonomic issues of defining what is rural and what is urban. Despite these drawbacks, the Goldschmidt hypothesis research is notable for its examination of the social consequences of agricultural industrialization, a topic hitherto ignored by rural sociologists (see Nuckton et al 1982, Harris and Gilbert 1982, Green 1985, Lobao-Reif 1987, Gilles and Dalecki 1988, Barnes and Blevins 1992, 1993, Gilles and Gilleta 1993, Lobao, Schulman, and Swanson 1993).

By the 1980s many rural sociologists were debating questions about American agriculture in terms of Marxian analysis (Newby 1978, Buttel and Newby 1980, Mann and Dickinson 1978, 1987, Mooney 1982, 1983, 1986, 1987, Friedmann 1978a, 1978b, 1980, Marsden 1986, Friedmann and

McMichael 1989). Further development of the Goldschmidt literature had by this time been limited by preoccupation with statistical techniques. Vail (1982) called for incorporating analysis of the political economy of individual rural communities into the 'Goldschmidt' research. Gilbert and Akor (1988) introduced the concept of 'logics of production' to compare statistics on capitalist farming in California with family farming in Wisconsin. Such a strategy broadened what had been a straightforward empirical question to a broader set of theoretical questions about the workings of capitalist economies. In so doing the question became more truly Goldschmidt's as it returned to some of his initial concerns not just with generalizations drawn from correlations between economic statistics, but on the relationship between production and policy operating to bring about such change.

'Industrial agriculture' is an empirical starting point for research just as any other industry, market sector, or geographic area might be in any society. However, the appropriate questions for social scientists to ask are not taxonomic - not concerned with specifying the requirements for membership in certain categories of that empirical realm. Rather, the appropriate questions are relational and systemic - what arises from the interaction of the various entities being observed, how does the pattern of interrelation change over time, what consequences does it have for society, and how do the mental models by which people negotiate their lives change in response to this system? These are the questions that Miner and Goldschmidt posed 50 years ago. These are also the kinds of questions that are best answered by models that attempt to parsimoniously mimic the empirical systems under observation, that attempt to conduct 'experiments', as Barth suggested, by comparison to a broad range of phenomena.

In the subset of the world economy that deals with production and distribution of foodstuffs no easy or clear-cut distinction can be made concerning the taxonomic status of any participants. No clear purpose is served by the endless debates in the Goldschmidt hypothesis literature over what constitutes family versus corporate farming. Inasmuch as reality is too shifting, the development of fluid generative models takes precedence over the establishment of fixed reference points. The NIE solves a dilemma in economics by developing models grounded in historical detail that weave together the varying motivations of choice with the constraints of emergent social structures and institutions. So too a 'new institutional' anthropology of agriculture must weave together an understanding of the historical emergence of the choices and adaptive strategies of food producers, processors, and consumers, with an understanding of the institutions which shape, to varying degrees, the nature of those choices.

What is called for at this point is a truly anthropological understanding of the entire institutional context in which industrial agriculture exists, starting with the way in which research and educational priorities contribute heavily to the overall structure of the system. This, in essence, is the rock which both Miner and Goldschmidt struck - they described too well the workings of a system of political and economic institutions. Those within the organizations bolstered by these institutions objected to the argument that their actions might contradict other, broader institutions associated with a democratic society. What the literature discussed here makes clear is that, as regards agriculture, the description of that process is largely incomplete but may have reached a critical point. The challenge is to push the study of industrial agriculture out of 'agriculture' and into the emerging study of institutions.

3 Case Studies of Two Networks

Introduction

In the previous chapter I described some of the theoretical and political controversies surrounding the anthropological study of economies generally and those economies based on industrial agriculture in particular. In this chapter I turn to the particular circumstances of my fieldwork in Iowa.

Starting in early 1995 I began studying the growth of cooperative swine production networks under a grant from Iowa State University's Leopold Center for Sustainable Agriculture. I studied two eastern Iowa networks in detail and collected data concerning a wide variety of other networks across the state. I was fortunate early in the study to gain the confidence of a veterinarian who, while recuperating from an injury, allowed me to act as his driver/assistant as he traveled to the farms in his area. This veterinarian was the organizer of a network described below and provided me not only access to his clinic and its customers but to the entire community of which he was a respected member. In addition to accompanying him on his daily rounds, I conducted numerous formal and informal interviews with farm families and attended meetings and social gatherings in the community. At the same time I was conducting interviews and attending meetings of another network in a nearby community. There my key informant was not only a farmer but also a member of the board of directors of a national pork producers' group. His experiences locally and as part of a national organization also provided many valuable insights into the structure of the rapidly industrializing swine industry.

Two practical and related issues confront household producers looking to cooperate to survive changes now sweeping the swine industry in Iowa. As large corporations move into a form of agriculture traditionally dominated by household producers, many are urging these producers to find ways to compete. Land grant university academics often argue that farmers are too independent, too uncooperative to work together - therefore they must be managed, their economic relationships must be governed by formal business organizations. At the same time, farmers often fear that even if they do cooperate it doesn't matter, the eventual dominance of swine production by large corporations is inevitable - whether these corporations are organized by outside investors or cooperatively by farmers themselves.

25

These issues are linked by a common conception of the economy based more on textbook theorizing than on empirical observation. In particular I question whether the creation of large-scale firms to organize agricultural production is either necessary or inevitable.

This book focuses on the emergence of swine production networks in Iowa. Using ethnographic evidence, I explore the successes and failures of several of these groups. The importance of these groups and the research on them is twofold. First, on the practical or applied level, understanding and communicating what contributes to the success of such groups enhances the opportunity for other farmers to imitate those groups. Second, understanding the emergence of cooperative economic strategies among farmers in late twentieth century Iowa will hopefully contribute to the broader anthropological understanding of cooperation and competition in other times and other cultures. In the next two chapters I present ethnographic information on the networks themselves. I then discuss a model of cooperation based on the ethnographic evidence. In later chapters I tie the ethnography to a broader view of the competitive structure of Iowa's swine industry. Returning to the theoretical issues discussed in chapter two I discuss the structural similarities between the models of cooperation and competition.

Pigs via Satellite

On a cold February night in 1995, I sat in a nearly empty junior college classroom listening to a satellite teleconference on networking sponsored by the National Pork Producer's Council (NPPC). The teleconference, nationally broadcast from Des Moines, featured a panel of speakers and video clips of swine producers discussing cooperative business ventures. The moderator assured us that hundreds of farmers across the Midwest were participating in the teleconference. All of them were sitting in rooms like this watching a television screen where speakers urged them to form networks in order to survive sweeping swine industry changes.

The overriding principle of the cooperative network, the speakers explained, was to improve the standing of its members in a way not available to them as individual farmers. They described several possible forms of networks: information sharing, joint purchasing, joint marketing, and joint production. All of these were based on function, what the network does, rather than how the network does it. Within each function were a variety of strategies. Although networks come in all shapes and sizes, from informal coffee shop discussion groups to corporations with multi-million dollar facilities, the message from the NPPC that night clearly emphasized the larger formal organizations.

The NPPC depicted networking as a survival strategy. In place of the 'mortgage lifter' sideline that hogs provided to traditional family farmers, many speakers foresaw hog farming as a specialized business enterprise, operated by professional managers and driven by economies of scale and the worldwide demand for pork.

'Change is coming' prophesied Glenn Keppy a farmer and past president of the NPPC. The message from the economists, livestock specialists, and producers that spoke emphasized such change and promised a bright future for those willing to embrace it. These experts and producers used the language of business schools - 'networking is the end product of a strategic plan,' intoned one, 'Total Quality Management' was invoked by another, another encouraged producers to develop 'mission statements.' All of the solutions were presented as part of a program to enable farmers to compete successfully in an industry increasingly dominated by large scale corporate interests.

If there was a hitch to this rosy prognosticating it was summed up by a farmer from Illinois: 'pigs are easy, people are a challenge.' Several speakers commented that 'people problems' would interfere with the best laid plans of managers and experts. An economist described the failure of similar networks two decades earlier due to the inability of members to get along.

The NPPC teleconference represented the best efforts of many academics, farm leaders, and producers to encourage a new kind of farming. As an anthropologist I wanted to find out whether this version of reality bore any resemblance to the actual experiences and ideas of swine producers who were attempting to cooperate.

During 1995 and 1996 I studied the problems and prospects of networking among hog farmers in rural Iowa. What I saw convinced me that networks have the potential to benefit farmers but not in the manner envisioned by planners who design networking strategies from office suites and lecture halls. If there is a people problem it is with the people who work from the assumptions of the agriculture schools rather than the realities of farmers.

The Top-Down Approach

Driving through eastern Iowa you come to understand the stylized landscapes of Grant Wood's paintings. The hills are rounded in an abrupt fashion, lined with corn in long straight rows just as Wood depicted them sixty years ago. If that part of the landscape resembles a Grant Wood depiction little else about rural Iowa does. Shiny metal grain bins, ranch houses, and trailers frequently replace the red barns and settlers' frame houses. Soybeans now share equal acreage with corn. Hog production has shifted from clover pastures to intensive confinement on many of the remaining hog farms. In February of 1995 I traveled through eastern Iowa to the town of Millersville to meet with Steve Longley, a farmer and organizer of a network (all names and locations are fictitious).

Steve, in his late thirties, had recently taken over his family's farming operation from his father, with whom he had worked since graduating from Iowa State University. With his wife Janice he raised pigs from a herd of 300 sows in a variety of confined and semi-confined buildings. Janice managed the confinement farrowing house and nursery where pigs are born and weaned, while Steve handled the outdoor finishing lots. In addition, Janice kept track of all of the production and financial records on the farm's personal computer. Because of the frigid Iowa winters in recent years, the rate of gain of pigs fattened on these outdoor lots had suffered. While Steve's new breeding stock produced lean animals that the packers paid premiums for, their lack of fat required the warmth of an enclosed finishing unit or they simply spent too much energy keeping warm instead of growing.

To solve this dilemma Steve began talking with nearby farmers about the possibility of forming a network to build new nursery and finishing facilities in order to modernize and expand their operations. After a few informal meetings Steve decided to seek some planning help from outside. The overall plan came from a group of advisers organized by the Extension Service at Iowa State University known as Team Pork. Team Pork operates as a consulting group through the Cooperative Extension Service. Farmers and networks must apply to receive assistance from Team Pork and only the largest and most progressive farms are deemed worthy of the group's expertise. Steve and his partners visited the Team Pork advisers in Ames and returned with a large 'Community Nursery Handbook' to help them develop their plans (Team Pork 1994). Like the NPPC teleconference, the handbook offered a sort of cookie cutter approach. Additionally, Steve

and his partners employed a business planner who worked for Land O`
Lakes, a regional cooperative in eastern Iowa, to help produce the plans for
creating a limited liability corporation.

All of the members of the group but two were clustered around the
nearby town of Millersville. Bill Craig, Jack Smith, and Al Jones had grown
up in this community. Al's partner, Brian Williams, was a transplant from
nearby Kelton. The other two members, Bruce Weber and Herman Mueller,
lived near Alton 30 miles to the north. They had heard of the Millersville
network plans through their veterinarian and started coming to the planning
meetings at Millersville after a network effort in their area failed.

The plan that Steve and the other farmers worked on all winter
called for building new nursery and finishing facilities. Pigs from each
member farm would go to the nursery facility at weaning then be
transferred to the finishers where they would remain until they were
marketed. The plan, Steve explained, was an ambitious one utilizing the
relatively new technology called segregated early weaning or SEW.

Instead of weaning pigs from their mothers at about six weeks of
age, typical of Iowa farms, the pigs are weaned at less than twenty one days
and transferred to 'hot' nurseries. These specially built nurseries provide
warmth, food, and water for the young pig until it is transferred to a
finishing unit for fattening. The pre twenty one day weaning is crucial as
this is when natural immunities from the mother protect the piglet from
disease. By removing the young pig from contact with older pigs, exposure
to disease is eliminated. This provides several key benefits to producers.
First, pigs are healthier, thus reducing the costs associated with medication,
veterinary expenses, and death loss. Second, rate of gain is improved
because of the better health. Third, the immunity allows the commingling of
pigs from different herds as the risk of disease transmission is greatly
reduced.

At the same time this new technique poses some challenges.
Isolation is crucial to SEW success. Baby pigs need to be moved to
nurseries that are not just in different buildings, but on sites widely
separated from the sows or older finishing pigs. The problem this poses is
that most hog farmers have traditionally located their facilities on a
common site, sometimes even in one building where pigs move from one
end of the building to the other in an assembly line fashion. The SEW
technology has been rapidly adopted by large corporate feeders who
construct new facilities on isolated plots of land with the needed separation.
Most family farmers by contrast don't have that luxury.

The dilemma Steve and his partners faced in financing their project was that a great deal of capital and managerial skills were going to be needed to put the planned facility together. In order to gain the efficiencies needed to utilize the SEW process, these farmers would be forced to abandon part of the production process traditionally performed on their own farms and become farrowing specialists. The project would turn the members into investors in the limited liability company that would own the facilities.

'In some ways,' Steve said over lunch at the Millersville Cafe, 'it would be easier for us to get a 30 or 40 million dollar loan than it is going to be to get three million.' He had been giving me an introduction to the complex world of financing a new hog production facility. I quickly saw that the image of the dungaree-wearing farmer borrowing money from local bankers on the faith of his word and the hope for abundant rainfall was in need of modification.

'Can your local bankers handle the smaller sized loan?' I asked.

'No they don't have the stomach for it, it's too much for them but not enough for the big banks. We may try to get money from private investors or by working with a leasing company to finance the buildings. If we wanted thirty million we could go to Rabobank, the Dutch bank that finances the big producers.'

Duly impressed by the scale of this proposed project, I sat in on a meeting in the basement of the local Lutheran church that afternoon while Steve and his partners discussed various aspects of their project. Financing was one of the chief issues and Steve reminded the group that they all needed to submit their financial statements to the group's accountant for inclusion in any loan applications. Rather than openly share their private financial information, the members agreed to provide that information to one of the many outside advisors they were using. Steve presented various spreadsheets depicting financial scenarios on a color monitor attached to his laptop computer. I struggled to keep up with the technical discussion of facility design. As I listened to this group of relatively young progressive farmers I was impressed with the calm, polite, argument free manner in which they discussed their plans.

A few weeks later I once again sat in the Lutheran church listening to Steve and his partners discuss their plans. By then, I had spent time getting to know some of the members individually. This night the basement was occupied by a church council meeting so the network meeting had moved to the sanctuary where the farmers sat uncomfortably on hard wooden pews. At one point the pastor looked in and joked about the juxtaposition of God and mammon.

By this meeting, I had learned that one of the members, Jack Smith, would contribute over half of the pigs to the proposed nursery and finishers. Jack, in his early forties, looked more like a suburban stockbroker, in his Ralph Lauren shirt, than an Iowa hog farmer. He produced pigs from over 1200 sows, many of which were tended by other farmers on a contract basis for Jack's farming corporation. As Jack told me later, he often felt he was 'helping out' these farmers who had suffered financial setbacks in hog farming and could no longer obtain credit but who were, nonetheless, skilled operators. The son of a hardware store owner, Jack had turned to farming after finishing high school and ran his operation from a modern office at the main farmstead. At the meeting, Jack's input was listened to attentively by the other members. Still, at this point, each member's opinion carried equal weight despite their differing financial stakes.

As the evening progressed, the conversation moved from topic to topic with little formal agenda. At times, the farmers launched into detailed discussions of the merits of building materials and genetic characteristics of swine. The meeting didn't end until well after midnight. By the end it was clear that the major questions about building design, scale, and financing had been agreed on. All that remained was to make a loan application. After six months of church basement meetings, the network appeared ready to begin.

What happened over the next few weeks came as a surprise to almost everyone. The first indication of trouble came when I finally arranged an interview with Herman Mueller. Herman was in his mid fifties and he and his wife Alice ran their farm with the help of a son. The Mueller farm, like the Smith farm, was immaculate - the kind of place where the road banks are mowed like a lawn for a half-mile in either direction from the farm house. Herman, a Vietnam veteran, dressed in traditional bib overalls, sat with Alice in the kitchen as we talked. Over the phone he told me he was planning to leave the network. Herman was a straightforward common sense operator who made it clear that he had no intention of signing a three million dollar loan. His reasons had nothing to do with cooperating with other farmers. Instead, Herman observed that he would be at the same risk as others but they would stand to gain more.

'To their credit they've heard the wake up call,' he said, but added that it was a call he had heard a long time ago. Herman characterized Bill and Steve, both of whom still finished their hogs on open lots, as operating in 'caveman fashion'. Herman had driven by both farms and considered their generally poor appearance as a reflection of the farmers who ran them. His own farm was an efficient confinement operation with little debt. Herman wanted to make it more efficient by converting his nursery and finishing units to more farrowing space and placing pigs in an offsite SEW nursery. Bill and Steve, Herman observed, hadn't made the same needed improvements as he had and now were faced with the need to frantically catch up. While the network would do that for them, it caused Herman to ask why he should be assuming equal risk for far less gain. The fact that they hadn't modernized earlier caused him to question their skill as managers. It wasn't so much that he didn't want to be in a network, he just didn't see how his farm fit with some of the others - their needs just weren't the same.

That same afternoon I drove down the road to Bruce Weber's farm and heard much the same story. Bruce was young and ambitious, but like Herman he shared a suspicion about acquiring a large debt and working with farmers whose needs were different from his own. Also, like Herman, he didn't harbor any ill will toward the Millersville farmers, but he noted that whenever a meeting was held it was clear that a number of issues had been decided beforehand. It wasn't that the Millersville farmers were trying push their own agenda, Bruce explained, it was just that they frequently saw each other at the church and the coffee shop, which resulted in conversations and decisions that he couldn't possibly be part of.

Within a few days, Herman and Bruce officially notified Steve Longley that they were leaving the Millersville network. Steve was disappointed but accepted their decisions without rancor and hoped to recruit other farmers to take their place. With Bruce and Herman out of the picture and the financing package ready to go, it became clear that the debt on the remaining farmers would be larger if they didn't scale the project back. Al Jones and Brian Williams announced that their participation was unlikely as well because of the increased debt burden. That left Steve and Bill, each with about 200 sows and Jack Smith with his 1200. If it continued, the network was going to have to alter its plans.

Network planning was put on hold until planting season was over. By early summer, Jack Smith announced that he too had decided against participating. Like the others, he reported that the needs of his farm didn't match with those of Steve and Bill's. A problem raised by all members, but especially by Jack, was swine genetics. Each farmer obtained breeding stock from a different source and each was loyal to a familiar brand. The process of commingling pigs was, among other things, designed to produce large numbers of relatively uniform animals in hopes of attracting higher bids from packers. The lack of common genetics would make that problematic. It would also raise problems with feeding because different genetic lines created variation in gain. Jack's large investment in breeding stock made him particularly unwilling to switch to the genetics preferred by Steve and Bill. It was on this point that the one member one vote rule was stretched too far for Jack. 'Why, if I have the most animals, if I contribute the most to the network, should I have to abide by the decisions of the people with so much less at stake?' Jack asked.

Jack's departure effectively ended Steve's networking project. One summer night I sat with Steve and Bill at the dining table in Bill's house as they discussed their options. All of the formal planning for the network was now largely useless and the two men discussed the possibilities for building a much smaller system on one of their own farms. As they tried to figure out a new arrangement, I began to see the flaw that had brought down their plans. Reviewing one option after another it became clear that Bill and Steve knew very little about each other's farms. From the type of facilities and their age, to feeding practices and ingredients, it was clear that both men were running very different operations. Lacking such knowledge they had substituted the top-down approach of the Team Pork plan instead of devising a system responsive to their own individual needs.

I was surprised that such details hadn't been covered months earlier until I remembered Steve's early description of how he selected farmers for the group: 'they were all progressive enough to accept the networking concept'. It wasn't a matter of selecting farmers because they had common needs, but because they seemed to fit Steve's image of progressive farmers - the same image that planners from the Ag schools apparently held.

Weeks later, still no closer to his goal of starting a network, Steve concluded that the network's failure was due to the independent nature of farmers. He characterized the farmers he'd tried to put together as similar to artists, each pursuing his own specialized vision of how a hog farm should be run. What really happened was that the organizer and members of the Millersville network didn't know enough about one another at the outset of their venture to adequately evaluate the plan foisted on them. Once they began to assess one another and their own needs, they found the network plan to be a poor fit. Comparative data from a second network illustrates why this happened.

The Bottom-Up Approach

Veterinarians, like other small town business operators have a great deal riding on the future of family farmers. The equity in a veterinary practice is generally considered 'blue sky', that is, the anticipated future revenue from a solid client base. Many vets base their retirement plans on the sale of that blue sky to a younger partner. With declining numbers of family hog farms, many vets worry about who will buy their practice down the road. For veterinarian Allan Garrison this factor was sufficient to motivate him to form a network. In addition, he saw networks as a way of preserving the small town in which he and his wife Kris planned to bring up their children.

Located near the Mississippi River in Kelton Iowa, the Kelton Pork network was already up and running when I first met Allan Garrison. Allan was in his late 30s, a partner in a six-member veterinary practice that covered several counties in eastern Iowa and northern Illinois. After attending an NPPC forum on networks he decided to try organizing a network among his customers. As he traveled around the countryside he took note of the various needs of individual customers. Building on this knowledge, Allan selected a group of farmers who needed to reduce the fat in their hogs to meet the new standards for leanness set by the packers. Rather than encouraging individual farmers to purchase better quality breeding animals, Allan urged them to pool their buying power to bargain with a genetics supplier.

A dinner meeting in the spring of 1995 marked the network's first anniversary. I sat with a group of farmers as we waited for dinner. Short stretches of conversation were punctuated by awkward silence. I finally had to ask if everyone at the table knew one another, the silence was so uncharacteristic of a group of farmers. 'No,' came the amused reply from a young farmer sitting next to me, 'but we're working on it.' The network had been formed with farmers from all parts of Allan's trade area and very few of them were acquainted. Unlike Steve Longley's failed network, which was made up mostly of neighbors, here was a successful network of strangers.

As the evening progressed, I learned that Allan had approached each of the farmers with the same pitch, getting together in order to meet a need. But rather than pick a group of farmers who were socially alike, Allan's strategy was to pick from two groups of farmers with complementary economic needs. The first group was made up of twelve farmers who needed to upgrade the quality of their product for packers.

These were younger, mostly small to medium sized farrow to finish producers, relying on family labor to run their farms. Although they needed new breeding stock, the cost of new breeding animals was too high compared to the traditional method of replacing breeding animals from their own herd. The other group was smaller, made up of three feeder pig producers with very small operations. These farmers had off farm jobs or businesses and only farmed part time. This group faced a dwindling demand for the small groups of pigs they traditionally sold through weekly public auctions at country sale barns. They also faced lower prices due to the small numbers of pigs they marketed.

Allan's solution was to arrange for the smaller producers to buy breeding stock from a genetics company and produce replacement gilts (breeding age females) to be sold as 40-50 pound feeder pigs to the group of farrow-to-finish producers. This provided a ready market at a premium price for the feeder pig producers and a source of improved genetic stock requiring only a small cash outlay for the farrow to finish producers. The genetics supplier, a small family run company, was willing to go along with the plan because of the volume. Allan described the network as a win-win situation for everyone. He was correct.

As I traveled from farm to farm with Allan, I came to understand how he knew the needs of his clients. Although individual farms varied enormously, their needs were not unique. As I listened to Allan discuss network arrangements with farmers it became clear that any belief in the virtues of independence was not impinging on their desire to be part of the network. They were making choices not following traditions.

Allan's network also had its share of defectors. But Allan had done two things to ensure that such defections didn't destroy the network. First, all of the farmers who were buying gilts had roughly the same size farm. Thus the network was not overly dependent on any one member. Second, the network not only had a large number of members but it also had a number of farmers waiting to join. I interviewed each of the farmers who defected and each told the same tale - the new breeding stock hadn't performed to their expectations. Allan admitted that there had been problems that he and the breeder were working to eliminate.

There are both social and economic dimensions at play. In Allan's network, the two dimensions complement each other, while in Steve Longley's network they worked at cross purposes. Allan had a plan with a clear economic benefit to all participants coupled with the social and cultural values that accorded him a trusted position as an organizer. Steve

Longley attempted to link a group of farmers based on social relationships rather than common economic need. As a farmer, Steve chose from a range of social acquaintances and had limited economic information about them. In fact, all of the farmers I met with knew very little about each other's farm operations. As one farmer put it, 'I don't know how my best friend raises hogs.' That lack of knowledge is explainable by the lack of financial relationships between farmers. In contrast, Allan Garrison has a firm economic and operational familiarity with farms that is important to his ability to provide treatment and advice.

The physical separation of individual farmsteads and the lack of communal economic activity, such as the threshing and baling crews of an earlier generation, produce farmers who are often less economically familiar with each other's farms. It is this economic isolation that renders sharing of information and cooperation difficult between farmers. Instead, intermediaries like Allan Garrison provide a link by identifying economic need while sustaining network cooperation through traditional rural values of trust and reciprocal need.

Making Alternatives Work

Allan Garrison contacted all of the same advisers that Steve Longley did. But rather than accept the top-down approach promoted by ISU's Team Pork and others, Allan worked from the bottom-up. In other words, Longley employed a plan developed without input from farmers while Garrison used input from farmers as the chief means to develop a plan. As I traveled across Iowa interviewing organizers and members of other networks a pattern emerged. Successful networks were organized by persons who knew a wide variety of farmers and knew the economic dimensions of their farms. They were also tailored to the needs of the members rather than to an idealized plan. Additionally, small networks such as Allan Garrison's reported little community opposition such as that provoked by large scale corporate facilities. The social compatibility with the local community is as crucial as economic compatibility within the network itself.

After Allan Garrison's initial networking attempt took off, he decided to try to expand the original network in two directions: 1) to add members to the original gilt multiplier network, and 2) to enlist some of that network's members in a new network to construct a segregated early weaning (SEW) nursery much like that proposed by Steve Longley. Most of the time I spent working with Allan was during the negotiation period for the SEW project. In this section I recount part of that experience in order to illustrate the effort that went in to planning this project as a bottom-up rather than a top-down initiative.

Allan had already started proposing the possibility of creating an SEW facility by the time of the first annual meeting of the Kelton Pork network. Following a presentation by network president Bill Kelley that recounted the network's history, Allan proposed a far-reaching set of goals for the network's future. He announced that a feasibility study for the SEW nursery had been started by the adviser from Land-O-Lakes who provided financial consulting and credit assistance to Kelton Pork and other networks. In addition, Allan told the farmers that he foresaw the possibility of Kelton Pork expanding to the point that it could market its own name brand line of pork products.

In the next chapter I discuss Allan's plans for retailing meat. Here I describe the complexity of Allan's negotiations with the members of Kelton Pork. The point of this discussion is to tie networks to the broader theoretical concerns of this book, particularly through the concept of transaction cost.

Every Wednesday afternoon Allan and I called on the Cable farm near Kelton. Don Cable was a bachelor in his mid forties who lived and farmed with his parents, both in their 70s. Although their farm bore few of the signs of the progressive farm so admired by agricultural journalists, it did, as Allan and others assured me, possess one key attribute – money.

The Cable's were old school farmers who worked sun-up to sundown and owed no one a penny. When a steel producer began buying up farmland for a factory in their area the Cables steadfastly refused offers of over one million dollars for their farm, forcing the giant company to change its plant's proposed location. If there was a stronger example of the legendary independence of farm folk in the area I never came across it. Yet at the same time the Cables were among the network's earliest supporters and eagerly awaited the start of the SEW network. Their hog operation would have made the members of Iowa State's Team Pork cringe. Not only did they lack a record keeping system more advanced than the stack of paper overflowing Annie Cable's desk, their sows were rarely farrowed on anything resembling a schedule. As a result their nursery pens and finishing building contained a mix of hogs of all sizes and ages. My visits with Allan took on aspects of a comic opera each week as Don leaned over the pens in the finishing building and asked Allan which hogs might be ready to take to market. Dutifully Allan looked at the animals and marked with a red veterinary crayon all of those he felt were sufficiently fattened. Following this selection all of us began to sort the market ready animals into separate pens using a combination of small wooden or metal 'crowding' gates, shouting, arm waving, and the occasional kick.

One July afternoon, following thirty minutes or so of this activity, we emerged sweaty and smelly from the finishing building into the cooler outdoor air for a drink of water from the nearby hydrant. This particular day was blessedly cool for pig and farmer alike. When temperatures climb above 95, as they had the previous week, hogs must often be sorted at night or early in the morning lest the heat stress on the fattened animals kill them. Following the sorting work in the farrowing house, the family usually gathered around the hydrant as we refreshed ourselves and as Allan and I began the process of scrubbing our boots to prevent diseases from spreading to the next farm we would visit.

As usual Don or his mother would ask Allan about some aspect of swine raising that they had probably asked ten times before but which Allan happily answered once again. Allan's patience with and solicitude for the Cables went beyond professional courtesy. He told me that when he had been hospitalized with a life threatening injury the previous summer, the Cables had brought fresh produce and baked goods for his wife and children every week. Today though it was Allan's turn and he brought up the subject of the SEW nursery. The first advantage for the Cables of being in the nursery would be that they could eliminate their own jerry-built nursery in the lower level of the nearby hay barn. Second, by participating in the nursery network, their sows would be on a regular farrowing schedule so that together with the other participants they could provide a continuous supply of pigs to the unit. Finally, such a schedule would result in deliveries back to the farm of uniform groups of pigs which would eliminate the arduous weekly sorting in the finishing building.

On one hand it might seem as if this plan was forcing the Cables into the kind of top-down straight jacket that caused the collapse of Steve Longley's network. Yet Allan's careful reading of the Cable family proved otherwise. As he explained the plan that afternoon, all three family members nodded their heads in agreement, especially Annie. The charming veneer of the tradition bound farm seemed to wear thin when Annie's role was examined closely. Responsible for all of the household chores, as women frequently are on Midwestern farms, Annie also worked side by side with her husband and son in the fields and hog barns. Already well past the age when many of her friends had gone to retirement homes, Annie was clearly frustrated with the never ending cycle of work.

What Allan saw in this family was the immanent shortage of labor as the aged parents would soon be able to contribute less time and effort to the farm. For them and their son, participating in the network made a great deal of sense from the perspective of the family cycle. Such observations are shared by many observers of peasant agriculture from Chayanov to John Bennett. The network 'fit' the Cable farm because it responded to the changes in available labor characteristic of a household production unit. The Cables were approaching the point on their drudgery curve where age and labor availability dictated a decrease in the size of their operation. The SEW network would streamline much of the work and allow the Cables to adopt a production system that required much less labor.

As the summer progressed Allan made similar pitches to other farms in the network. Although each case had its own particular needs Allan could see the rationale behind a switch to the SEW nursery. Once enough farmers were willing to seriously discuss the issue of building the SEW Allan began a series of formal meetings to discuss the specifics of the venture. The most important question to be resolved was whether the group would construct a new facility or attempt to rent an existing one. One of the problems that Steve Longley encountered was that by having elected to build a new facility early on in the planning process (and having enlisted Team Pork to design the physical, operational and financial aspects of such a project) he had committed the group to a plan from which it was difficult to disengage. At Allan's meetings, in contrast, very little was set in stone other than the principle characteristics of the SEW process itself.

Outside of the formal meetings Allan used his weekly herd health visits to ask prospective members for off the record comments on the proposals. Like the prospective members of Steve Longley's group, the Kelton Pork members were reluctant to dissent during meetings. Only in these private conversations did they make their true feelings known. One such case was that of Carlton Baker.

In his early fifties, Carleton was by far the wealthiest member of the group. He farmed over 2000 acres of the county's best farm ground and his home and farmstead were showplaces. Yet rather than opt for a new facility as one might have expected of a prosperous progressive farmer, Carlton was urging Allan to look into leasing an existing facility. Like many survivors of the 1980s farm crisis, Carlton had learned caution. One morning at Carlton's farm, Allan mentioned that he had been contacted by a farmer in the neighborhood who had declared bankruptcy the previous spring and whose hog facilities were available for lease. Carlton's reaction was one of immediate relief. The plan to build a new facility had called for the members to assume equal responsibility for a $400,000 debt and Carlton was uneasy about that prospect.

Allan mentioned the leasing possibility to the other farmers and they expressed similar sentiments against acquiring a debt laden new facility. Yet none of these farmers, so debt averse in private, had ever expressed such reluctance at group meetings. This demonstrates one of the most difficult aspects of organizing a cooperative network. In effect, what I was witnessing in Allan's attempts to negotiate a consensus on whether to build or lease a facility was the persistent cost of negotiating and transacting. Each member had to be approached individually to elicit his true feelings. Each would rather share those feelings privately with his trusted advisor Allan, than publicly among his peers. The reason for this reticence was somewhat elusive, but seemed to lie in the direction of both not wanting to appear uncooperative or lacking in the 'guts' to undertake a risky venture – something of a combination of Midwestern politeness and male ego. That Allan was able to successfully negotiate this minefield was due to the structural advantage he possessed. Not only did his position in the community earn him the respect of prospective members, it also greatly lessened the cost to him of obtaining information. Another organizer would have been at a disadvantage similar to the hapless anthropologist with his clipboard and questionnaire attempting to solicit information at a much higher cost than the well connected veterinarian. This was the root of Steve Longley's difficulty, the cost in time and effort of determining the physical and operational characteristics of his neighbor's farms (let alone the social cost of prying into their state of mind) was just too great. In Longley's case, he arguably 'didn't know what he didn't know'. However, the access to information is the central issue. What limits access is the effort that must be expended in obtaining that information. Garrison's advantage is that, by virtue of his position in the social structure, his cost both of 'knowing' and of 'knowing what to know' is reduced.

Despite his advantage in obtaining information about the network's prospective members, Allan was not immediately successful in bringing the SEW network into being. Although the planning started in early 1995 and numerous subsequent meetings held, the network was not functioning when I revisited the group in the fall of 1996.

On a cool evening I sat on the screen porch at network president Bill Kelley's house while the negotiations continued. Determined not to try to control the situation Allan sat on the edge of the group listening. The planned lease of the facility from the bankrupt farmer had fallen through because of legal technicalities. Over the summer Joe Willits, one of the original Kelton Pork members, had proposed renovating his existing farrow-to-finish facilities in order to become the nursery operation for the group. His proposal was a straightforward per head production contract similar to that used by other contract hog producers. Joe's wife Denise worked part time in their current farrowing and nursery operation and this move would create a full time job for her while freeing more of Joe's time for crop production. As Carlton Baker noted during the meeting this plan had enormous advantages for the group, particularly in the area of personnel. Were they to build or lease another facility the network would have to employ workers and managers and establish an agreed upon method of monitoring performance. Joe Willits, on the other hand, was a respected farmer whose skills no one doubted either in group meetings or private interviews.

On Bill Kelly's porch, numerous questions were raised about Joe's compensation, production scheduling, ownership of the pigs at various stages, and liability for poor performance or death loss. Not wanting to exert a decisive influence, Allan let the group come to its own decisions, but at the cost of longer negotiation time. The particular sort of cost this delay entailed was in lost profitability. The longer the members debated the fine points of their alliance, the more pigs they raised individually without benefit of the new nursery.

Allan estimated that participation in the nursery would save $7.00 for every pig produced. Using a conservative estimate of 18 pigs per sow per year on a farm with 100 sows, a one year delay in getting the facility up and running would cost each farmer over $12,000. This 'opportunity cost' can also be described as a transaction cost inasmuch as it resulted from the numerous negotiating delays brought about by the bottom-up organizing process. Additionally, as they came closer to drawing up formal contracts with Joe, this negotiation translated into higher legal and accounting fees. The course of time will prove whether this carefully crafted arrangement is more sustainable than the cookie cutter networks that have been created elsewhere.

In comparison to Steve Longley's failed network it seems that such care is rewarded. The real issue is whether the internal sustainability of the network, purchased at the price of the lost time and revenue that the negotiations entailed, will be enough to counteract the broader economic issues confronting Iowa's hog industry.

4 Case Studies of Other Networks

In this chapter I briefly describe ten other networks I studied following my work with the two networks described in the previous chapter. These networks came to my attention through word of mouth and were selected opportunistically. They do, however, represent a broad variety of networking strategies and several areas of the state of Iowa. In most cases I interviewed the organizers of each group rather than individual members as I had done with the previous two networks. The groups discussed cover the gamut from new networks struggling to get off the ground to mature organizations dealing with the problems of aging facilities and members. In addition, some of these networks have experienced the growing controversy over the environmental effects of industrial swine production first hand. My goal in this chapter is to provide not only further details about the organization and functioning of networks among Iowa's farmers, but to also lay the groundwork for a broader understanding of where networks fit in the swine sector of Iowa's agricultural economy. Also, by expanding the analysis outward beyond the organizational structure of individual networks I will further address the theoretical issues raised at the beginning of this work.

Clinton Quality Pork

Clinton Quality Pork typifies the large-scale top-down model of network organization and function. In 1991, John Davenport, then feed sales manager of Clinton County Cooperative, a large feed and grain coop, in Taylorsville, IA, began the process of putting a swine production network together. Much like veterinarian Allan Garrison, Davenport traveled around the countryside putting together a list of farmers whose farms would be compatible with a 2400 sow farrowing and nursery center. Davenport worried that Clinton County Coop, a Farmland Cooperative affiliate, would eventually lose much of its feed sales base if a competitive alternative to the large corporate owned facilities could not be found. In addition he saw many farmers and their families taking part-time jobs off the farm. 'Our goal was to find them an off-farm job *on* the farm,' he explained.

Like many other organizers, Davenport, in reflecting on the failure of the 1970s sow coops, felt that ownership and management of the new network facilities should be strictly separated. The network would provide pigs ready for finishing to the individual farms where members would construct new facilities in accordance with the production requirements of the network. Management and labor at the network facility was to be provided under contract by Clinton County Coop. Financial and organizational planning were contributed by Farmland Cooperative.

In Davenport's view, the most difficult aspect of putting the network together was obtaining financing for the project. The group contacted Jim Kenny, a local financial planner with a background in agricultural lending at Farmers Home Administration. Kenny reviewed in confidence the financial statements of prospective members to determine their eligibility for membership in the network. Local lenders however were skeptical. 'It was too big for them,' Davenport noted. In the end the network obtained its financing from the same Denver based bank that financed Clinton County Coop.

The network members boasted that they had been able to obtain their loan with only a 30% downpayment and no personal guarantees. In actuality those terms were only obtained because the members agreed to buy pigs from the network at a price that always guarantees the network a profit. In other words, although they are not personally liable for the debts of the network, they are contractually obligated to keep the network solvent (in effect guaranteeing the loan) by paying whatever price the network management charges for its pigs.

When I met with members of the network in the summer of 1996, the nursery was nearing the start of what is called its first 'turn', the completion of one cycle of production. The members of the network were excited about the prospects of finally getting production in full swing. However the story they told about the costs to them personally reflected a much different experience.

The network's facility generated considerable controversy in the Taylorsville community. The network members began to feel the social pressure from indignant community members, farmers and townspeople alike, in numerous ways. Terry Richland replaced John Davenport as the project manager after Davenport left Iowa to head a Nebraska based coop. Richland, who had grown up in Taylorsville but spent many years working in the Chicago offices of Continental Grain, described his surprise at the intensity of the opposition the group encountered. 'These guys were hand picked,' Richland told me, 'they were community leaders - school board members, church council members.' Over lunch the members of Clinton Quality Pork acknowledged that their lives had changed as a result of constructing the facility. Their children were taunted at school, lifelong friends quit speaking to them, they were refused service at some restaurants. Then there were the late night phone calls - abusive calls that Richland and all of the members reported receiving. 'When I worked for Continental and we were building these things in Missouri,' Richland lamented, 'nobody knew who I was or how to find me in the Chicago office. Now they know my home phone number.' Despite the difficulties, the members of the network are determined to see their project through. Looking intently at me over the lunch table, Lyle Nelson, one of the older members of the group stated matter of factly about the network's opponents, 'At some point we just said 'fuck 'em, we're gonna do it'.

PigProfit

The PigProfit network was the brainchild veterinarian Jerry Nagle. Nagle planned to build a large sow facility known as a 'gilt multiplier' to supply breeding stock to member farms. His story in many ways parallels that of Clinton Quality Pork but with a much different outcome. While Clinton Quality Pork was located in sparsely populated southwest Iowa, Nagle's network was to be located in the rolling hills of eastern Iowa near Cedar Rapids, an area dotted with the rural homes of urban workers. One opponent that Nagle particularly resented was a former state legislator who had been instrumental in bringing large scale swine production to north central Iowa but who now opposed it in his own backyard. Opposition became so intense that many of Nagle's prospective members backed out.

In the end, Nagle and his remaining members, determined to bring their network into being, purchased an existing farrowing facility and its sow herd to use as a gilt multiplier. They planned to gradually replace the existing herd with improved genetic lines from a new swine breeding company. However, lacking a solid member base to subscribe to the breeding stock, the PigProfit network was forced to market its replacement gilts to nonmembers. PigProfit found itself in competition with many other breeding stock producers. The group's competitive difficulties increased when, due to a glut of breeding stock on the market, prices for gilts began to fall. At the same time, one of the local coops began a network among its members, further draining members and sales from PigProfit.

Nagle could have thrown in the towel as financial difficulties mounted and he and the network's members were forced to contribute additional capital to the venture. Instead he began to notice opportunities among the farms where he was trying to sell breeding stock. Many farms had excess finishing capacity and were looking for SEW pigs which could be safely commingled to fill that capacity. Other farms and networks had excess SEW pigs to sell. Nagle found himself acting as a broker between these parties.

From eastern Iowa the trade area for his brokerage quickly expanded across the U.S.. The day we met he was putting the finishing touches on a deal to ship SEW pigs from Montana to Pennsylvania. Impressed with the success of his brokerage efforts Nagle began other networks that responded to the direct needs of his customers. He started several small information sharing groups, as well as a marketing network. Over all he noted that he was quite surprised by the way things had gone, 'It's not what I expected, but it works.'

Much like Allan Garrison, Nagle discovered the value and profit to be derived from having a structural advantage in the flow of information between several disconnected individuals. Looking back he characterized his early mistakes as having come from not listening to the producers before making firm plans for the network. Nagle also disparaged reliance on outside consultants or those with a vested interest in seeing the network succeed. Much more useful he felt were efforts based on listening to producers and filling a need than trying to impose rules from outside. He had transformed and adapted his 'network' to fill a unique niche in the industry. It might have been a far cry from that envisioned by the consultants from Iowa State University who originally advised him, as Jerry Nagle recognized, it worked.

Nagle also described experiences that parallel those of other networks. In an attempt to put together a marketing network Nagle contacted the offices of a nearby IBP plant. He negotiated a premium price for the finished hogs from the members' farms based on delivering truckloads of high quality lean hogs. Since all of the hogs were of a similar genetic makeup the farmers were willing to accept the average price for the whole group as the price for their own production. Problems began immediately. Nagle claimed that the field buyers for the packer felt that they had been cut out of the deal and that more deals like Nagle's would jeopardize their jobs. The field buyers studied the kill sheets (the packer's quality assessment of each animal killed which determines the prices paid to the farmer) and identified several farmers whose pigs would have brought more than the group's price when bought according to their own grade and yield characteristics. They then approached these farmers and persuaded them to leave the marketing network in order to get a higher price.

Farmers whose hogs were below average had been getting a far greater premium than they could have earned on their own. As the top producers left, the group's average quality fell to a point where the packer would no longer pay a premium to the group. The marketing network eventually disbanded. At the time we last talked Nagle was trying to put a new marketing group together by picking farms whose quality would vary so little that the temptation to defect from the network wouldn't be a problem.

A similar fate befell a buying group that Nagle attempted to put together. Realizing that the farmers could experience significant savings on livestock feed and supplies bought in quantity from regional distributors rather than local retailers, Nagle tried to create a network to buy from one of these distributors. Like the marketing group this network was plagued with defectors. The local retailers merely went to the largest farmers and cut their prices to match those of the distributor. Without enough volume from the remaining farmers to support the large purchases, the network collapsed. Again the lesson Nagle recommended to other network organizers was to be sure to group together farm of nearly equal size in order to prevent defectors. As with the marketing network and Allan Garrison's network, the key lies in matching the needs of the network members as closely as possible.

Vinton Pork

On the bookshelf above Mary Vinton's desk is a copy of George Gilder's best selling book *The Spirit of Enterprise*. That title in many ways characterizes Mary's approach to farming and networking with her neighbor's. Mary's office, unlike most farm offices which are located in the farm house, occupies a storefront in downtown Wellington, IA. From there she manages the production record keeping and accounting for the operation she shares with her husband, the farmers who are contract finishers for Vinton Pork, and several other farmers who pay for her record keeping services. This activity puts Mary in a position similar to Allan Garrison's - she knows many important details about farms in the area and often serves as an information conduit between farmers. According to Mary there are four farms like the Vinton's in the Wellington County area that control most hog production through contract farming arrangements. Not only are the contracting farms dependent on maintaining the financial stability of the four large operators, but so too is much of the area's agricultural economy.

Mary Vinton's father was a John Deere dealer in western Iowa. She grew up always knowing she would have some sort of career in agriculture. After graduating from Iowa State, she married and moved to her husband Duane's family farm in the early 1980s. She and Duane expanded his father's sow herd from 350 to 1200 sows over the next several years. Although there were good years, there were also many financially stressful ones. As their debt mounted and credit became increasingly difficult to get, Mary and Duane began to look for alternatives to building new production facilities on their own farm. One of Duane's cousins had gone out of the hog business but was left saddled with empty facilities he couldn't pay for. That was when Mary and Duane started contracting production in order to expand their own operation.

Mary noted that by 1994 three other large producers in the county had started similar programs. In the fall of that year the four large farms began discussing the possibility of a joint marketing venture. Altogether the group accounted for 160,000 finished hogs per year worth between $17 and $20 million. They approached Cargill's Excel Packing in Kansas City and negotiated a contract guaranteeing a minimum price for their production, the terms of which are confidential. One of the farmers in the group emerged as the leader and spokesperson, but it was Mary who maintained the channels of communication in the organization.

All seemed to be going well until the week the contract was to be signed and Mary got a call from Excel. The farmer who was the network's spokesperson had contacted Excel privately and asked for a contract for his own hogs only, effectively cutting out the other members of the group. Mary noted that even the Excel buyers seemed surprised at this turn of events. Because the defector controlled nearly half of the hogs in the network there was very little the rest of the group could do. Eventually they renegotiated their own separate contract with Cargill and the marketing network came into being but not without straining what Mary described as an intricate network of overlapping business, family, and social ties in the community.

Reflecting on the experience of her own networked farm with its subcontractors, as well as the larger marketing network, Mary offered a number of observations for other would-be network participants. First, she dismissed the advice from Iowa State's Team Pork as irrelevant. She described their networking strategies as akin to arranged marriages in their attempt to impose structures and rules. She also noted that she was disillusioned by the frequent lack of honesty between farmers at group meetings. She attributed this partly to male ego – many of the largest farmers refused to admit to poor performance or mistakes. But she also attributed it to the competition between the large farms for land and for contract producers. This competition exaggerated the sense of isolation and secrecy that each family felt. She noted that the farmer who defected from the network was still allowed to attend the group's information sharing meetings. At a recent meeting he had dominated the conversation in an attempt to convince the rest of the group that they should be more candid with one another about their performance. Still skeptical Mary remained uncertain whether the needed honesty would emerge.

Wellington Feeder Pig

Another group of Wellington County farmers established Wellington Feeder Pig in 1994. Wellington County has traditionally been one of the largest producers of feeder pigs in Iowa but the changing structure of the industry has greatly reduced the county's output in recent years. Wellington Feeder Pig was established to provide its members with a consistent supply of feeder pigs in the face of the declining market. Bob Duncan, a local feed mill owner, was the catalyst for the group, utilizing a structural advantage similar to Allan Garrison's to recruit members. The group built a 1200 sow farrowing facility run by a full time manager and three employees. Even though the Wellington Feeder Pig operation looks like many other large networks, Duncan scoffed at many of the 'package' networks that were being offered by the large coops in the area. He felt that the Wellington network had been carefully designed to fit the needs of its members rather than something they had to buy into.

The Wellington network has also had its share of community and internal difficulties. Located close to the town of Wellington, there have been many complaints from local residents. A local veterinarian I spoke with characterized one of the members of the network as 'the town bully' who had intimidated the residents with plans to expand his own facilities even closer to the town. This farmer subsequently claimed to have received an anonymous death threat. Duncan confirmed that the network had had its share of trouble both in the community and internally.

In the last few weeks before the construction plans for the facility were finalized, lacking the needed capital, the group decided to accept two members who were, in Duncan's opinion, bound to disrupt the group. While Duncan had attempted to pick members who had experience in leading community groups and who farmed in partnership with family members, the two late comers were much less experienced in shared decision making. Duncan noted that these two members frequently interrupted the discussions over trivial points and expressed dissatisfaction unless all of their own demands were met.

Another interesting aspect of the Wellington network has to do with Duncan's reason for starting it. Duncan noted that he wanted to build a farrowing unit because he felt it was more profitable for farmers to be in the finishing business. 'As everyone knows,' he told me, 'the money in hog raising is in the finishing end.' What is interesting about this comment is that only a few days prior to this I had been talking with Allan Garrison whose plans were just the opposite – keep the farrowing on the farms and move the nurseries and finishers off the farm. Allan's comment was just the opposite of Duncan's: 'as everyone knows the money in hogs is in farrowing.'

Feeling somewhat confused by what 'everyone' was supposed to know I decided to consult the experts at ISU. I located an extension publication that advised farmers on what type of hog production system was the most profitable (Lawrence 1995). Based on surveys of several farmers, the report concluded that neither farrowing operations alone nor finishing operations alone were as profitable as a combined farrow-to-finish operation. In other words no one seemed to be able to agree on what everyone was supposed to know – the veterinarian, the feed salesman and the economist all claimed to 'know' where the money was in hog feeding. I bring up this example from the Wellington network in part to note the 'mental accounting' which colors farmers' assessments of their farm's performance. I also suggest that the differences between Duncan's and Garrison's estimates may have something to do with what each wants from the network. Duncan, despite all of the effort he put in to organizing the

Wellington network, was not rewarded with the farrowing center's feed business. At the same time he did retain the members as customers for finishing feed which constitutes a much greater tonnage. Similarly, Garrison could be replaced as the veterinarian for the SEW nursery if the members so chose. At the same time he hopes to retain the individual farms as customers. But the amount of veterinary work involved in a farrowing operation is far greater than that involved in nurseries or finishing operations. Neither Duncan nor Garrison said anything to suggest that they were making these kinds of calculations. I merely note that the logic of each man's perception of what constitutes profitable hog raising for his customers seems to correspond to the arrangement that best suits his own purposes as well.

Valley Pork

Valley Pork started in northeast Iowa in 1976 as one of the feeder pig coops that were popular in the 1970s. In 1994, when farmer Brian Tulley was offered a chance to buy shares in the facility, three of the original seven members were still involved in the business. Tulley explained that he was unfamiliar with the facility or its members until he was approached by his feed salesman. He began attending meetings and eventually decided to buy into the facility in order to assure himself a steady supply of feeder pigs for his finishing operation. Although he was concerned about investing in such an old facility, Tulley was much more comfortable with the size of the investment required in Valley Pork as opposed to a new venture. Since he joined the group, construction started on a new SEW nursery to complement the farrowing unit.

Buying into an established network can often be a complex process. Brian Tulley's investment had to be approved by all of the members in the group rather than just the individual selling the shares. The members of Allan Garrison's SEW network included similar requirements in their network agreement. Although this strategy gives the existing members some ability to screen out troublemakers or financially troubled members, it also limits the value of shares due to their lack of ready marketability. In the case of the Valley Pork network, Tulley described two brothers whose shares in the network had been for sale for over a year but who could find no buyers. Tulley characterized the two as troublemakers who always complained about the quality of the pigs they received even though other members had no complaints. The two had not attended a meeting of the group for over a year. At the last meeting they attended they walked out after announcing that they were selling their shares. Tulley described with some amusement the reaction of other members who realized the unlikelihood of the brothers making good on their threat.

Tulley had been warned about the brothers behavior before joining. With 40% stake in the network and as its largest member, Tulley worried about his ability to influence the direction of the network. This problem occurred in other networks as well. Some, such as Clinton Quality Pork, required members to invest equal amounts. In these cases one share equaled one membership which equaled one vote. Despite the variation in the size of each investment, many other networks operated the same way. In Brian Tulley's case he had the legal right to vote 40 out of 100 shares, but in reality the voting authority was shared equally by the members. When the farmers in Allan Garrison's SEW network were negotiating they came to a similar conclusion – in the event of serious disagreement everyone had the right to vote according to the number of his shares. However, as a practical matter the network would operate under the one member one vote rule.

This extra-contractual reciprocity is not confined to farmers in Iowa. The legal scholar Macaulay noted in his classic article on non-contractual relations in business that many transactions occur outside of formally agreed upon specifications (Macaulay 1963). The situation in many networks seems to be tailored to the particular social situation rather than the specifics of the contract. In the case of Steve Longley's network, Jack Smith refused to join because he could not be assured that his voice would equal his contribution, i.e. that his contractual rights would prevail over the decision making rules of the group. In Brian Tulley's case he joined because he realized that his voice would prevail over the dissenters who had been dismissed by the rest of the members as cranks. In short the formalities of network agreements in these cases seemed to take a back seat to the interpersonal negotiations between members.

PorkPro Artificial Semen Center

One of the biggest issues for many networks is whether to organize as a 'profit center' or a 'cost center'. In essence the question is whether the network itself should make a profit which it returns to members as dividends or whether the network should just break even and by doing so help the members increase the profit of their own farms. Many network members prefer the latter alternative, directly improving their farm's bottom line. Many lenders prefer the former alternative as it tends to guarantee loan repayments. The members of Clinton Quality Pork recalled the amused look on their banker's face when they proposed backing a $2.5 million loan with a cost center approach.

PorkPro Artificial Semen Center faced many of these issues when it was being organized. Bob Duncan, who organized Wellington Feeder Pig, also helped put PorkPro together. The network owns a single small facility known in the swine industry as a 'boar stud'. The facility houses several boars owned by various breeding companies. An employee regularly collects semen from the boars which is then either picked up or shipped by overnight delivery to farmer customers. Sows are then artificially inseminated (a process known as AI) on farm. This technique is a step beyond the traditional mating of animals by placing boars and sows in the same pen when the female is in heat. It is also a step beyond the way in which AI is practiced on many farms. The switch to AI from conventional breeding requires a fair amount of technical training for the farmer. In addition, boars are expensive, aggressive to handle, and their fertility must be monitored frequently. Boar studs have become popular by addressing problems associated with an on-farm AI program. Rather than maintaining boars and sows, the farmer concentrates on handling sows and leaves the complications of semen collection to the boar stud.

Farmer Mark King, who helped Duncan organize PorkPro, saw the semen collection business as a service to farmers in his area. He wanted to establish the boar stud as a cost center. 'What good would it do the industry to build another profit center?' he asked during an interview. King and Duncan managed to convince a group of sixteen local farmers of the soundness of the plan and of its benefits to their operations. The group leased land from one of the members who agreed to work in the facility they would build. The sticking point for the members was the requirement by the lender, Farm Credit Services, that all of the investors provide personal guarantees on the loan as a condition of operating as a cost center. In the end the condition was met but King reported a number of late night phone conversations and considerable effort to convince some members. The result of this arrangement had some rather odd repercussions. Like the Valley Pork network some members of PorkPro became dissatisfied with the operation of the network, especially when an unforeseen sales shortfall required the members to advance additional capital. King recalled a meeting where one member stormed out announcing he was selling his interest in the network. After he left the rest of the members reflected on the likelihood of selling shares in a concern that didn't produce profits. This problem was compounded for all of the members by the fact that the business also sold semen to non-members thereby negating any reason for someone to acquire shares in the venture. 'I guess we all realized we would own these shares for life,' King confessed.

Why did King and the other members invest in the network in the first place? King described their motives as partly the self-interest of buying semen at below the going market rate and partly the desire to provide a service to other farmers. This seeming altruism was not entirely unusual when I compared PorkPro to other networks. Organizers in particular often seemed to be less interested in their own profits than in the long term health of the industry and their communities. It was assumed by Allan Garrison and Bob Duncan that any direct pecuniary motive on their part would convince farmers that their networking efforts were a sham. Better to benefit the system of which one hoped to be a part than be perceived as too overtly feathering one's own nest. At the same time Mark King's professed altruism didn't entirely hold up. Recall that the boars in the boar stud were owned privately. The owners charged commercial rates for the semen and paid PorkPro for maintaining the animals and collecting semen. PorkPro passed its costs along to farmers without taking a profit but the boar owners were not as altruistic. King and another member were distributors for a breeding stock company and as such owned some of the boars in the facility. While some of the farmer members may have had altruistic motives it wasn't entirely clear that all of them did.

Conway Pork

Conway Pork, like Valley Pork, was located in northeast Iowa and started in the 1970s as a sow cooperative. By the 1990s it had changed ownership several times and was most recently owned by a group of outside investors who sold feeders pigs from the farrowing facility. In 1994 Kevin Jones, a feed salesman with the local Land O' Lakes Cooperative, heard that the facility was for sale. Jones brought together a number of local residents to form a network as a limited liability company (LLC) and make an offer on the facility. Working much like other organizers through his personal network of sales contacts Jones was able to put together the farmers and the financing to complete the deal.

Like other networks, the Conway Pork network attracted members for a variety of reasons. Three of the eight members were family-based hog producers, two were retired farmers who no longer raised hogs, one was the manager of the network's farrowing facility, and two were a husband and wife who had been part of the previous investment group. The husband and wife also owned a large swine genetics company that sold gilts to the network. According to Jones, the three farmers had all borrowed the money to make their investment. The manager had done the same, a case of buying one's own job like many small business or franchise owners. The husband and wife retained their stake. The two retired farmers, who were actually the closest thing to true investors, expressed their feelings that they wanted to keep their money in the local community. In describing their motivation for joining neither mentioned return on investment as a primary factor. Both wanted to help younger farmers, such as the three local producers, stay in the business.

This community spirit also helped to explain Kevin Jones's original involvement in the network project. When we first met, Kevin asked me to help him come up with some statistics that would show how much hog farming contributed to the local economy. He was hoping to get the local newspaper to publish an article that would remind concerned area residents of the economic importance of the swine industry. Kevin argued that the survival of small towns like Conway depended on keeping hogs in the area. While he appreciated the arguments of industry critics that the number of producers in a given area rather than the number of hogs might be key to economic survival, he felt that the only way small farmers would survive was to band together to become big farmers.

Jones also saw the large cooperatives as being the natural leaders for this movement to farmer owned mega-farms. 'Privately owned agribusinesses just don't have the same resources we do in the cooperative,' Jones explained. He described the variety of technical experts he had called on for assistance as key to the network's success and to the retention of the feed account by the local coop. Not only were animal nutrition and health consultants available through the coop, but financial consultants were also available to assist in obtaining credit. The involvement of the cooperative also helped reassure lenders of the soundness of the network's operating plan. In addition, Land O' Lakes provided farmers with access to information from other networks in the Land O' Lakes system. 'It isn't a step by step process yet,' Jones noted, referring to the many details to be worked out when negotiating a network agreement, 'but we'd like to get there.'

Harrisburg Network

One of the commonalties I've noted between successful networks has been the presence of an organizer who was familiar with a wide variety of farms in his or her area and could therefore design workable combinations from those farms. This implies that the position of the organizer in the local social structure is sufficient for success in organizing a network. The contrast between Allan Garrison and Steve Longley would seem to support such a conclusion. However, the next two networks illustrate the problems that can be encountered by even a well-positioned organizer.

In Harrisburg, Iowa Stan Bailey and Marshall Reynolds were respected successful veterinarians. Like Allan Garrison they provided their clients with a progressive herd health program and became proactive advisors to many hog farmers. When the two decided, like many other vets, that their own professional careers might depend on forming networks, they sought out the best advice they could find. Both were graduates of the Iowa State University's Veterinary School and it was to their former teachers and to the school's multi-disciplinary advisory group Team Pork that they turned for help. The consulting group provided the vets with their large 'Community Nursery Handbook' that Allan Garrison had once dismissed as useless. They also provided detailed cash flow and budget analyses.

I attended a meeting of the Harrisburg group shortly after Team Pork had made its initial presentation to the farmers. At this meeting the farmers reviewed the material from Team Pork as well as listened to presentations from two lenders and an attorney. The lenders described the merits of financing options from their respective institutions and the attorney provided information about alternative forms of business organization. Only five farmers were at this meeting, a disappointment to Bailey and Reynolds since nearly 30 had attended the initial gathering. I asked why they thought so few retained an interest in the project and both replied that the two million dollar price tag had scared most away. Of the group attending the second meeting, two farmers seemed to lead the discussion, two participated somewhat, and a fifth sat off to one side of the room and said very little. The presentations by the attorney and bankers were fairly technical and the questions from the farmers focused on a variety of very particular issues. The two farmers doing all of the talking seemed very enthused by the project while the others seemed noncommittal at best. Bailey described all of the farmers as 100-200 sow producers, with primarily out door facilities who were looking for a way to bootstrap themselves into a modern production facility. Although no commitments were made at the meeting the general tone suggested that the core group was still interested in pursuing the project once certain details could be ironed out.

When I spoke with Stan Bailey a few weeks later his story had a familiar ring. All but one of the farmers had dropped out of the picture, most citing the large financial commitment necessary to participate in the network. Stan was frustrated that even those who had expressed optimism for the project had backed out. Despite his familiarity with each farm and despite the obvious benefits to the farmers of being involved in the farrowing complex project, the networking attempt had fallen apart. When I asked him what his strategy was at this point Bailey expressed continuing faith in the project. He explained that through his connections with a large regional feed company he hoped to bring in outside investors to build the facility. If one or two local farmers joined, so be it, but the farrowing center would be built to sell pigs to large commercial finishing units outside of the Harrisburg area. I asked if he had considered scrapping the Team Pork designed project altogether in favor of something on a smaller scale that might appeal to the local farmers, but he dismissed the idea. 'I guess I just want this more than they do,' he said.

The difficulties experienced by Bailey and Reynolds in Harrisburg illustrate how an organizer's advantage in the local social structure can be lost by imposing a top-down model on would be participants. Bailey and Reynolds, like Team Pork, operated from a set of assumptions about how the swine industry should be structured and what was needed to bring small farms into line with that structure. That the local farmers didn't share that view or that they resisted taking the financial risk needed to embrace it was attributed to their backwardness. But even being sensitive to the particular needs of every farm is often not sufficient when attempting to organize a network as the following case illustrates.

Anton Network

In Anton, Iowa Don Smith runs a two-man veterinary practice out of the offices where his father once practiced veterinary medicine. Unlike Bailey and Reynolds who were transplants in Harrisburg, Smith was a native with lifelong friendships and business ties in the Anton area. When I first spoke with him in early 1996 he was optimistic about plans for putting together a network. Although he hoped to encourage his customers to build a large farrowing facility he was open to helping them tailor any networking approach to their specific needs. By summer his hopes had faded and he was discouraged about prospects for the future. Echoing Kevin Jones's comments, Smith described the efforts of the local coop to organize a network. 'They have a package and they have someone who can devote all their time to pushing it.' By contrast he was unable to devote the needed time to the network and still maintain the busy schedule that his practice demanded.

In some ways Smith's case was the opposite of that of Bailey and Reynolds. In a way he knew too much about his clients and, lost in that particularity, he couldn't push for a common goal. He described how all of the potential network members he talked to recognized the need to be able to compete with the mega-producers, but each in his own way felt that the open ended networking alternatives Smith was exploring entailed too much risk. In addition to the coop's package network a number of contract hog feeding options were being promoted in the area by feed companies and large swine producers. Competition for pigs was increasing for those producers who relied on buying feeder pigs rather than raising them, but Smith noted that few seemed worried about their survival. 'It's simpler just to go out and buy it [pigs] rather than go through the cost and risk of networking,' he noted. This is a classic transaction cost issue. Cooperation entails numerous costs in terms of time and the risks involved in measuring and enforcing compliance. Similarly, Smith's own limited resources precluded his ability to spend time negotiating the cooperative transaction. The advantages held by the coop, the regional feed companies, and the contract producers overwhelmed Smith's ability to compete with the alternatives.

The Pig Palace

Like the previous case, the final network case study illustrates some of the difficulties that emerge for networks and network organizers outside of the would-be network itself. In Don Smith's case I suggested that other outside firms had a transaction cost advantage over Smith. In the following case outside influences again overwhelm the attempt to organize a network but here the issue is how transaction costs are increased by the exercise of political and economic power.

As I mentioned in Chapter 3 Allan Garrison planned a third network beyond the gilt multiplier and SEW projects. Garrison discussed with IBP officials the possibility of identifying animals that originated from the Kelton Pork network and selling those under a private label. His plan was to ship animals in great enough quantities that it would be worth IBP's time to sort and package products for the network. In many ways this plan is more complicated than it would seem at first glance. Packers can and do track individual carcasses through a processing plant and can identify the grade and yield of each carcass. Hogs are bought from farmers on this basis. On the other hand these plants process thousands of animals daily and, according to the IBP officials Garrison spoke with, it would take perhaps as many as 250,000 animals to get the company interested in such a scheme.

Despite the daunting task of organizing production on such a scale, let alone the marketing problems, Garrison persisted in his dream of marketing pork from farm to consumer with as few intermediaries as possible and with a greater percentage of the value of the meat returned to the farmer. All of these planning efforts came to a head (and possibly to an end) one night in June of 1995. Garrison, a gregarious and well-connected entrepreneur, arranged for a meeting of several people he hoped could help get his dream off the ground. The meeting was held at the farm home of Harold and Jean Burkhalter.

Burkhalter is a bit of a farmer eccentric, a tinkerer who likes to build and repair his own farm machinery, a restorer of antique cars, and a man, like Garrison, who dreams of a different ways of doing things. Among the guests Garrison invited were several local farmers, three bankers, Steve Longley, a state senator, a representative of IBP, advisors from Cooperative Extension and the Iowa Institute for Cooperatives at Iowa State University, and a representative from the office of the Governor's Economic Development Commission.

Although Garrison had organized the meeting, it was Burkhalter who gave the presentation of his ideas for forming a retail marketing venture he called The Pig Palace. The idea was that local farmers would take control of the sale of their products at the retail level by building a chain of markets that would sell pork products. The products would be identified as originating from family farms, sold fresh or cooked rather than frozen, and grown without the use of antibiotics or growth hormones. IBP or some other packer would kill and cut meat for the group but the retail operation would be theirs. All of the attendees at the meeting had been invited to help participate in obtaining a grant from the state for a feasibility study for the project. Burkhalter and Garrison's hopes were to eventually create a farmer owned cooperative to get their idea to market.

Burkhalter's presentation was low key and somewhat apologetic. He showed the group some sketches his daughter had drawn to illustrate what the retail stores might look like. When he finished the short presentation he asked his guests for their input. While I expected to hear some criticism of what was clearly an overly ambitious project with fairly naïve assumptions about the effort and risk involved, the response was surprising. One by one the guests took turns shooting down the idea. The IBP representative was the first to attack the plan, pointing out that one IBP plant killed over 12,000 hogs per day and that it would require a very large business to immediately begin selling that much 'fresh' meat. He also asked what Burkhalter had meant by residue free – was he implying that IBP's meat had drug residues and did he really expect IBP to process for them if that was their insinuation? Steve Longley also joined the discussion with a number of questions meant to discredit Burkhalter's idea. Longley, who at the time was still convinced that his own mega-farm network would succeed, was clearly skeptical of an attempt to challenge the status quo. He began citing statistics from NPPC studies concerning optimal line speeds for packing plants, retail-wholesale spreads, etc.

Burkhalter and Garrison listened passively as one speaker after another pointed out the problems with the plan. After half an hour of this the discussion began to turn more to the politics of family farming versus corporate agriculture. The IBP representative grew defensive as the farmers in the room began to complain about the poor profits available to them. Burkhalter tried to point to other cooperatives that had entered processing markets for agricultural products but the conversation verged on becoming a shouting match. The representative from the Economic Development

Commission said nothing and glanced at his watch as if looking for an opportunity to leave.

Finally, in a firm deep voice, the local state senator spoke up. The senator was himself a part time farmer but tonight his sympathies were elsewhere.

> We talk about this all the time in Des Moines...whether we can do anything for these small farmers, but I don't think it's possible. These big outfits are the most efficient and the little guys just can't compete.

With that the verdict seemed to be in on the Pig Palace.

Most of the guests left in short order and Garrison and Burkhalter were left shaking their heads at the response. 'We're gonna go through with this whether IBP wants in on it or not,' Garrison vowed. Burkhalter was clearly dispirited by the response. I expressed surprise that it was Steve Longley who seemed to lead the attack. Garrison complained that the point of inviting Longley to the meeting had been to show the support of the National Pork Producers Council, of which Longley was a board member. Instead the project had been scuttled. The representative from the Economic Development Commission, from whom Garrison hoped to get financial support, had left without comment.

At first glance, both Garrison and Burkhalter appear incredibly naïve. They clearly had invited the wrong set of players to this meeting, the presentation was amateurish, and the discussion got out of hand. Their performance here resembles Steve Longley's eventual failure in organizing his own network. I argue that it is in fact the same structural dynamic at work. In the process of organizing a network of farmers, Garrison possessed a structural advantage in the flow of information in his community, an advantage that worked to lower the transaction costs of organizing a network. Longley, by comparison, seemed hopelessly naïve, given his own poor understanding of the needs of his prospective members. In the same way, Garrison's attempt to organize the retail venture as a set of alliances between various players failed because of his lack of relevant information about the players. Garrison was a relative outsider to the state bureaucracy and the packing industry. His efforts to persuade these parties to join his efforts failed in part because of his inability to understand their motivations for participating in the system. It may very well be that a packer such as IBP has no interest in encouraging the efforts of groups such as Garrison's. The IBP representative may have been sent to the meeting to help scuttle the plans. Steve Longley also had motivations that were not apparent to Garrison. This disadvantage in knowing the needs and motivations of prospective allies led Garrison into an attempted relationship that failed. In chapter 8 I return to this issue to discuss the structural similarities between cooperation and competition.

5 A Model of Cooperation: Networks and Social Structure

Introduction

This chapter provides a worm's eye view of networks themselves, how they are organized and what contributes to the success of individual networks. The case study data from the networks described in the previous two chapters is assessed to develop a model of the organizational characteristics of swine producer networks.

All of the networks studied reflect four key organizational characteristics:

1. operational goals of the network itself - what function does the network serve for its members?

2. level of organizational complexity of the network - how does the network go about fulfilling its function?

3. characteristics of member farms - what kinds of farm operations are linked together by a particular network?

4. role of the network organizer and the flow of information within the network - who organizes and coordinates the activities of the members?

These four categories provide a common descriptive frame for all of the networks I studied. Below I explore the importance of these aspects of the networks. I then explain the success or failure of networks in terms of these categories.

Network Operational Goals

One seemingly obvious but often overlooked characteristic of producer networks is their intentionality – they are goal driven organizations. Unlike typical 'social' networks that emerge from interactions of individuals, these producer networks are consciously created. In other words a 'network' in the sociological sense is often a series of connections between individuals who may or may not be aware of each other and whose behavior as a group does not possess an articulated goal. The producer networks, on the other hand, are more properly described as formal organizations than as

63

networks. The goal is simply the operational purpose of the network – gilt multiplier, SEW nursery, etc. Because the producer networks are goal driven the important question for members and organizers alike becomes, who sets the goal, and who defines the purpose of the network?

In the case of networks that have been organized in a top-down fashion, the choice of an operational goal for the network is made in advance by the organizers and their advisers. Examples of this form of organization are Steve Longley's network, Clinton Quality Pork, and the Harrisburg network. Members are then selected on the basis of the organizer's perception of their compatibility with the goals of the network. Other networks have been organized in the bottom-up fashion where the goal of the network is worked out according to the needs of the members. Examples of this bottom-up organizing are Kelton Pork, Garrison's SEW network and the revised PigProfit.

The variation in networks demonstrates the potential for networks to tailor their goals to members' needs. Although many networks intended to use segregated early weaning to enhance their production efficiency, each approached this technology differently. Some retained the existing breeding lines on member farms, while others chose to establish a uniform genetic base prior to establishing an SEW nursery. Some hoped to capture further productivity gains by building new finishing facilities in addition to the SEW nurseries. Others contributed pigs to the nursery but returned pigs to individual farms for finishing. Members of several groups planned to increase the size of individual breeding herds once the new facilities replaced existing on-farm facilities. Although some groups are further along in planning the specifics of marketing projects many networks also see the future potential of networking to provide marketing benefits. Most see these activities occurring in the future.

Level of Organizational Complexity

The second characteristic in terms of which all of the networks could be described is their organizational complexity. Organizational complexity can be defined according to: scale and membership requirements, formal organization, facilities requirements, management requirements, labor requirements, financial requirements, purchasing plans, and marketing plans. Groups with similar goals may choose to operate at vastly different levels of complexity. Allan Garrison and Jerry Nagle both initially chose to organize gilt multipliers but Garrison chose a relatively simple organization while Nagle intended to use a much more complex form.

Table 5.1 compares several characteristics of the complexity of Kelton Pork and Steve Longley's proposed network (tables follow page 69). Kelton Pork, in attempting a greater number of projects with more members, seems to be a much more complex organization in many ways. The only area where Longley's network presents greater complexity is in the size of its capital requirements which reflects the larger physical scale of their project. Once again the choice of a top-down or bottom-up organizing strategy will influence the level of complexity. In many case organizers were far more willing to embrace a complex organization than were members who often opted for keeping the network simple. This was particularly true of financial characteristics.

Characteristics of Member Farms

The third way to describe networks is by the characteristics of their members. This is an area where the strengths of the organizer were particularly important. Failure to understand the particularities of individual farming operations could lead to incompatible combinations of farmers and network failure. Characteristics of members that organizers particularly need to consider are: attitude toward networking, age, family status, herd size, genetics and breeding, feeding programs, record keeping, herd health, labor availability, marketing plans, and available facilities.

Table 5.2 once again compares the Kelton Pork network with Steve Longley's. As I argued in Chapter 3, the Kelton Pork network succeeded because its members had several key operational characteristics in common even though they were all relative strangers. Longley's group, on the other had, though made up of a group of close friends failed because they had certain production-related conflicts.

Role of the Network Organizer and the Flow of Information Within the Network

Perhaps the most significant difference between the networks described above is the role of the organizer in obtaining information about the needs of each member. Some organizers have advantages over others due to their structural position – veterinarians being a clear case. Others may have the same structural advantage but fail to make use of it. Despite their differences and varying degrees of success the most important fact is that organizers were present in all of the networks I encountered. Networks, in other words, don't just happen. They come into being because one person acts as a catalyst, particularly with regard to the flow of information about and between prospective members. Table 5.3 outlines the differences between Steve Longley and Allan Garrison as organizers.

Toward a Model of Cooperation

In this section I present an explanation of why some networks fail while others succeed. My explanation of network success involves three key points. Network success is based on:

1. Identifying and linking farm operations with characteristics that are compatible with the operational goal of the network and with each other.

2. Identifying and linking farm operations with characteristics that are compatible with the organizational complexity of the network and with each other.

3. The presence of a network organizer who acts to identify and link the farms involved in the network.

Based on my observations of networks, I argue that the compatibility of the farms involved sets the conditions for the success or failure of a network. However, it is the organizer, whose knowledge and selection of participating farms influences compatibility, who bears the greatest responsibility for the success or failure of a network. As such network organizing is highly information dependent. Further, observations suggest that the role of organizer may best be filled by a non-farmer. Farmers, despite fairly dense social networks and connections to one another, frequently know very little about the operational characteristics of each other's farms. Veterinarians, such as Allan Garrison, often have more intimate knowledge of an individual farm than do the close friends or neighbors of the farmer. At the same time, many network participants expressed reservations about efforts of feed companies and other input suppliers to organize networks. The advice and activities of input suppliers is often considered suspect since they have something to sell. A veterinarian, on the other hand, is generally perceived less as a salesmen than as a trusted advisor.

One other interesting observation about potential network participants emerges from this perspective. The ability of the organizer to make compatible combinations of farms implies that the farm operations themselves are sufficiently malleable to make finding this compatibility possible. Paradoxically, producers who have devoted more time to improving the breeding stock and facilities base of their operations may present more unique difficulties than the 'average' producer. The average producer with a small investment in breeding stock and facilities can join a network with little risk or cost. The 'progressive' producer, the producer who has expanded his operation both in terms of improved genetics and modern facilities, may have more difficulty finding a network of compatible farms or in benefiting from a network. While the data collected here only suggests this possibility, it remains an intriguing one: large scale progressive family farms may be 'locked out' of networking arrangements by their commitment to progress and their own success. Networks may be more likely to succeed among the small to medium size farms that have failed to adopt many of the recent improvements in swine production technology.

In this chapter I identified the major characteristics relevant to the success of networks: 1)the compatibility of individual farms with the operational goals and organizational complexity of a network, 2) the social compatibility of the farmers involved in the network and 3) the role of the network organizer and the flow of information in the network. Of these three areas, operational and organizational compatibility are central. However the key to connecting the compatibility lies with the network organizer. The role of the organizer, which is the ultimate 'social' factor, is the key to the success of a network. Much like an entrepreneur, the network organizer rearranges the factors of production to achieve new combinations. Successful networks will hinge on the ability of key individuals with detailed local knowledge to identify and link farms and farmers into compatible combinations. Rather than imposing top-down organizational strategies which leave farmers with few choices short of conforming to a predetermined plan, the bottom-up organizer constructs a range of compatible choices for prospective members.

Those who ascribe network failures to the independence of farmers do so by failing to understand the complex characteristics and needs of individual farms and farmers. Farmers 'depend' on a vast network of input suppliers from breeders to equipment manufacturers to veterinarians. The larger network exists because farmers readily accept the benefits of improved production technologies. In order to succeed, network organizers must become as skilled as input suppliers in identifying an appropriate market segment and meeting its needs. A similar challenge exists at the state level. Policy makers, extension advisers, and others must recognize the complexity of networks and avoid one-size-fits-all recommendations. Just as the key to effective organizing on the local level lies in acquiring 'local knowledge', so too does organizing at the state level. The range of operational goals and organizational complexity available to networks precludes top-down prescriptions which ignore local context.

The role of those agencies charged with fostering agricultural improvement in Iowa should be to aid farmers and network organizers in collecting and distributing the kinds of information that can make successful networking possible. During the summer of 1996, under a grant from the National Pork Producers Council, two networking handbooks were prepared. The handbooks, one for network organizers and one for members, are intended to provide the participants with a useful set of questions and guidelines for forming producer networks. These handbooks were created and tested using input from the members of several networks. They aid in implementing the explanatory model of network success developed above. Network members and organizers can use the handbooks as workbooks to collect relevant information about a network and its members. I argue that this model of network organization provides a more useful set of guidelines than the top-down prescriptions devised by groups such as Team Pork and the regional cooperatives.

Key to this model of cooperation and to the practicality of the handbooks is the argument that networks succeed when information is exchanged between the members and the organizers in as efficient a manner as possible. Those networks that succeeded did so in part because everyone involved understood clearly from the outset what was involved in putting the network together and how it affected them. Those networks that were less successful were often plagued with misleading or incomplete information. The goal of the network handbooks is to imitate the organizational strategies of the most successful networks and translate this model into a practical tool for others. The first step in the handbooks asks members and organizers alike to specify what the operational goals of the network will be and to set a time frame within which they will be implemented. In observing the interactions between farmers and organizers it often struck me that there were great differences in their perceptions of what the network's purpose would be. The handbooks address this issue as the first level of information to be shared between organizers and members. My hope is that the sponsors will make the handbooks widely available to those persons interested in forming networks. I argue that it is farmers and network organizers themselves who stand to benefit the most from the use of this tool and that their participation is crucial to forming the kinds of links in local communities that can lead to successful networks.

Table 5.1 Organizational complexity of Steve Longley's network and Kelton Pork compared.

	Longley network	Kelton Pork
Members	2 members remaining; originally 6	11 members; new group of 15 members joining
Organization al Form	no formal business organization initially; limited liability corporation (LLC) planned	no formal business organization planned for gilt multiplier; LLC for SEW nursery
Facilities	Large scale; new construction	Existing or renovated facilities
Management	Not clear; group met irregularly with no fixed agenda or time table for meetings	board of directors in place, management team planned; regular meetings with agenda and time limit
Labor	Not clear; probably hired labor	gilt multiplier labor by members; SEW hired labor
Capital	Leasing company; $2.5 million for new facility	Remodeling of member's facility
Purchasing	Joint purchase of feed inputs; genetics independent	purchasing common genetics in gilt multiplier; joint feed purchases for SEW; individual or joint purchases for farrow and finish; possible custom feed product
Marketing	Not clear	individuals market own production

Table 5.2 Characteristics of farms in Longley network and Kelton Pork compared.

	Longley network	Kelton Pork
Operator's Age	most 35 to 45	most 35 to 45
Operator's Education	most high school	most high school, some college
Off Farm Employment	None	none
Community	Most one community, 2 from nearby community	3 from one community, several other communities represented
Places of Trade	wide variety of local businesses, many long term relationships	wide variety of local businesses, many long term relationships
Producer Organization	most very active in swine producer and other ag organizations; one NPPC board member	all members in various ag organizations, varying degrees of involvement
Type of Production	all farrow to finish; one member sells breeding stock	all farrow to finish with the exception of the gilt multipliers
Herd Size	varies from 100 to 1200 sows	little variation; average size is 100-125 sows
Facilities	all have confinement farrowing and nursery with outdoor finishing; 3 producers with some confinement finishing	majority have confinement farrowing and nursery with both confinement and outdoor finishing

Table 5.2 - continued.

Sites	majority have one or two sites; one producer with ten sites	Majority have one or two sites
Genetics Used	variety of brand name lines	Formerly home grown replacements; currently all using one type of gilts; wide variation in boars, moving to same boars
Breeding Techniques	majority AI	Majority natural breeding
Feed Program	wide variety of suppliers; most using split sex and phase feeding	Wide variety of suppliers; most use phase feeding, some use split sex feeding
Production Record Keeping	most using computerized record keeping for sow herd and production records	Some used computerized record keeping, primarily for sow herd; several keep no production records
Vet Used	four original members use vet in their community; two use vet in nearby community	all use vet who organized network
Herd Health	all have experience with a wide variety of diseases; PRRS present in one herd	all have experience with a wide variety of diseases, currently no major disease problems
Labor	majority use family labor, one wife involved, some hired labor	Majority use family labor, several wives involved, little or no hired labor

Table 5.3 Flow of information in network.

	Longley	Garrison
Level of Acquaintance	original members and organizer reported higher levels of acquaintance with one another than with members from nearby community	members reported on the whole low levels of acquaintance with one another; organizer reported high levels
Frequency of Visits To Member Farms	all members reported few visits; organizer few visits	all members reported few visits; organizer is frequent visitor at all farms
Level of Familiarity With Member Farms	original members reported high level of familiarity with each others farms, little with members from nearby community	members reported little or no familiarity with each other's farms; organizer reported and demonstrated high level of familiarity
Requests For Information	most members reported organizer as likeliest to request information	most members reported organizer as likeliest to request information; several reported exchanges with other members
Sources of Information	most members reported organizer as likeliest source of information	most members reported organizer as likeliest source of information; several reported exchanges with other members

6 The Changing Nature of Swine Production in Iowa

Introduction

This chapter reviews recent changes in swine production in Iowa. Like much of the developed world, the agricultural economy of Iowa has been subjected to radical restructuring as political economies driving institutions and policies reshape traditional family farming. The latest act in this drama is being played out in the swine industry. In the past 20 years, 70 percent of hog farmers have left the industry. In Iowa alone, the number of swine producers has declined over 40 percent in the last 15 years, twice the rate of general farm decline. Nonetheless, total swine production has remained relatively stable (Iowa Agricultural Statistics 1996). In place of small family operated farms, where hogs provided a sideline to cash grain farming, new production strategies such as vertical integration by corporations and contract farming are rapidly expanding.

As a result of these political economic shifts as well as new production strategies, Iowa is witnessing a demographic shift as a growing rural working class emerges to labor in factory farms and packing plants. As contract production expands many formerly independent farmers are reduced to the status of propertied laborers performing 'disguised' wage work not subject to either minimum wage laws or fringe benefits. Locally, many rural and small town economies are threatened by the relocation and concentration of swine production to a few areas in the state. Those areas face social and environmental risks that accompany the influx of immigrant workers and pollution from hog wastes. Capital is increasingly fed into swine production not from local sources but from regional and international lenders. Proponents of these changes include packers, non-family corporate producers, politicians and many in the agricultural schools of land grant universities. The land grant universities in particular provide the ideologically and politically motivated science to justify this increasingly controversial restructuring (see the discussion of this politicization in Chapter 2).

Recent changes in the organization of swine production in Iowa are causing widespread concern that family farms will be driven out by large

74

vertically integrated producers. In response, many farmers are joining the cooperative networks described in previous chapters. The meaning of the term network in local contexts varies considerably. Agricultural extension advisers from Iowa State and other land grant universities promote networks as formal business organizations. Others involved are clearly exploiting the situation, such as the feed salesman I overheard attempting to enlist a farm couple in a contract production scheme - 'you've heard about networking,' he said, 'well I'm here to tell you about networking with Cargill'. It is difficult to imagine Cargill, the largest agribusiness corporation in the world, 'networking' with family farms.

Despite confusion over the use of the term network I encountered several examples of new types of alignments among swine producers. In some respects these alignments appear to be confounding the attempts of either the state or agribusiness interests to transform household based agricultural production into business firms. Not only are these fluid informal relationships beginning to show signs of stability, but they even make the possibility of networking with Cargill less ludicrous than it might appear at first glance.

In this chapter I discuss how networks may become one of the key strategies used by family farm swine producers as they confront the political economy of industrial agriculture. I attempt to demonstrate that networks constitute a viable adaptive response on the part of household producers to the rapidly industrializing swine industry. The challenge in attempting to understand any new economic arrangement is to sort out the competing interests involved and their relationships. The effort to promote small cooperative networks of hog farmers in Iowa has taken on much of the flavor of civic virtue, an assumption that such endeavors will bring widespread benefit. I also look at some of the participants in Iowa's swine industry who have taken a direct interest in promoting these cooperative arrangements among farmers. In particular I consider what benefits may accrue to the various participants in this system. I look at the interests of five groups – hog farmers themselves, corporate hog producers, existing farmer cooperatives, packers, and the state.

Swine Production In Iowa: An Overview

In post World War II Midwestern agriculture swine production occupied a part of the general diversified farm. In early spring sows gave birth in small wooden shelters on pastures where they remained with the young pigs until summer. At that time pigs ready to be fattened were placed in pens near the farmstead. Manure and bedding were spread on nearby fields during the winter. When fattened these hogs were trucked to a nearby sale barn where they were auctioned to the highest bidder from a handful of meat packing companies. Labor was primarily provided by the farm family. Occasionally a farmer preferred to specialize in just the breeding and farrowing aspects of the production process and sold young pigs before they were fattened. Other farmers who preferred only to fatten hogs purchased these 'feeder pigs'. Once again the local sale barn provided the meeting point for buyer and seller.

The 1970s was a period of transition for swine raising. The boom in grain prices, subsequent land speculation, and agricultural and economic policy, fueled a general get big or get out mentality in agriculture. Advances in antibiotics and equipment design made possible the construction of confinement swine production facilities. Many farmers built small to medium sized facilities to raise pigs indoors. Many early facilities combined three stages of the swine growing cycle under one roof: farrowing, nursery or growing, and finishing. By keeping this process under roof farmers began to farrow their sows on a year round rotation. The confinement swine production farm took on the trappings and advantages of assembly line production. The process was fraught with risk for early adopters, many of whom encountered serious disease problems not seen in the outdoor feeding system. In addition, the need to service heavy debt loads for new facilities made it much more difficult for farmers to decrease or exit production in response to low prices or changes in the availability of household labor.

During this time, large packers such as IBP increased their efforts at direct buying from farms, circumventing the sale barns which declined steadily in numbers. At the same time farmers began to regard the feeder pig auctions as risky affairs because of the spread of new diseases fostered by intermingling animals from different farms. Farrow-to-finish operations isolated from outside herds became synonymous with a well-managed swine operation.

The late 1980s and early 1990s saw further changes in the organization of swine production. Refinements in technology and advances in veterinary science led to greater success in controlling diseases. Many began to realize that the proximity of several classes of animals - i.e. breeding stock, sows farrowing, newborn pigs, and pigs in various stages of fattening - contributed to health problems. The solution seemed to lie in physically separating the animals at each of these stages not just to different buildings but to geographically separated production sites. This latter adjustment posed a problem for many swine producers. Unlike capitalist firms which often plan for a fixed-life production facility, farmers, living on the same sites where they engage in production, often assume much longer periods of usefulness for their buildings. Farmers found themselves faced with the need to abandon or extensively remodel facilities, which were often not yet paid for, in order to achieve production efficiencies necessary to pay for increased capital costs.

Compounding these problems was the rise of large vertically integrated swine producers. Backed by large sources of capital, these firms built production facilities on a scale which dwarfs even the largest family farms. Not constrained by residence and multi-generational landholdings, these firms built production sites in numerous locations to maximize the isolation of one phase of production from another. In the process swine production changed from an ecologically and socially integrated aspect of household production to an industrial process which can be subdivided and rearranged into its component parts purely on the basis of swine biology.

The Emergence of Corporate Swine Production

Recent changes in hog production in Iowa can be understood by examining public records from the Iowa Department of Natural Resources (DNR). DNR requires all livestock producers who use open-air manure storage facilities to register those facilities and file an approved manure handling plan. The status and regulation of such facilities has been the subject of much debate in the Iowa legislature. Local residents, who have experienced the powerful stench of these open-air manure storage facilities, have complained bitterly about the effect of such facilities on their health and quality of life. One recent study raises the possibility of a link between respiratory tract ailments and residence near a large confinement facility (Thu *et al.* 1997).

DNR, as of the end of 1995, recorded 548 applications for these lagoon or basin type facilities, all but 30 of which had been granted permits and were either in operation or scheduled to come on line shortly.

While these facilities are owned by a small fraction of the estimated twenty five thousand hog producers in Iowa, they are significant for a number of reasons. First, the controversy over large-scale hog production in Iowa erupted as a direct result of the construction of many of these facilities. Second, many in the industry have expressed their belief that such facilities are the wave of the future and will come to dominate hog production. Third, despite the small number of producers and facilities represented, the percentage of the state's hog production coming from these facilities may be quite significant. The DNR data records only the 'liveweight capacity' of each facility. This is an estimated figure based on an average weight of animals. The meaning of the figure varies depending on whether the facility houses sows, growing pigs, or finishing pigs. Since the DNR records do not specify the type of production at each facility it is impossible to make an accurate estimate of the proportion of Iowa's swine production contributed by these facilities.

The data has been geocoded for use with Geographic Information System (GIS) software. GIS provides a means of layering information tied to specific geographic regions in order to visually reveal patterns from tabular data. In addition to the basic information on hog farms, Iowa DNR has made available several other coverages ranging from political boundaries to environmental features (figures and tables in the following discussion follow page 89).

Figure 6.1 shows the 588 permits granted and their location for each year from 1987-1995. Table 6.1 summarizes the building activity over the nine year period. The greatest period of building activity occurred in 1994 when 30.7% (168 permits) of the total number of all permits representing 36.5% of total capacity were granted. Figure 6.2 demonstrates the growth of the largest facilities relative to the smallest and average. Figure 6.3 shows the relative size of the facilities in the state. What these figures and table make clear is a pattern of not only increasing numbers of facilities, but of a tendency toward rapid growth of the largest facilities and their concentration in two areas of the state – north central and northwestern. The largest 25% of facilities account for 53.8% of the total liveweight capacity built while the smallest 25% account for a mere 9.1% of capacity of facilities built. Wright, Hamilton, and Hardin counties in North Central Iowa are home to 36% of the liveweight capacity of all the facilities built in Iowa during this period.

This development presents a striking contrast to the traditional distribution of hog farms in Iowa, a distribution which seems to correspond more closely to the ecology of Iowa's farmland. Figure 6.4 shows the major geologic regions of Iowa layered with the facility locations of Figure 6.3.

The north central area of the state, which has seen the largest growth in intensive hog production facilities, contains the Des Moines lobe, a region of broad open fields and poorly drained soils formed in the last ice age. The farms of the Des Moines lobe have been key grain producers in Iowa while livestock has been concentrated in the steeper less productive soils along Iowa's eastern and western borders (for a description of Iowa landforms see Prior 1991). Figure 6.5 shows the distribution of hog farms in Iowa from the 1992 Census of Agriculture. These maps illustrate the traditional regional adaptation of livestock production in Iowa and the stark contrast presented by the locations of many of the new facilities. One explanation for the traditional pattern is that it reflects an adaptive response by farmers to their respective environments. Where soils were good and grain production profitable farmers specialized in the cash grain monocultures that developed during and after the Second World War. Where poorer soils proved harder to till and contributed to more variable grain production farmers responded to this uncertainty by diversifying into livestock production. Why then, as Figure 6.4 suggests, have the largest of the new hog farms suddenly appeared in the midst of a traditional grain growing region?

One answer may be found in Figures 6.6 and 6.7 Using records from the Office of the Secretary of State of Iowa, I was able to determine ownership of each of the facilities listed in the DNR database. Four hundred owners were identified for all but seven of the 588 facilities. I then classified ownership according to form of business organization – sole proprietorship, partnership, cooperative, limited liability company (LLC), and corporation. For corporations and LLCs I further broke the classification down by examining the lists of officers and directors in the corporations' filings with the Secretary of State. All but nine of these entities could be classified. Corporations and LLCs where one surname predominated as directors or officers were classed as 'family corporations', while those with multiple surnames were classed as 'non family corporations'. In addition, based on ethnographic and other documentary sources, some corporations and LLCs were classed as 'networks'. In this group are companies owned by several individuals with different surnames but which can be distinguished from investor owned or other non-family companies by the fact that many of the owners appear to reside in the same community as the facility in question. Many of these groups were contacted during the ethnographic portion of this research and also identified themselves as networks.

Figure 6.6 shows the distribution of the various forms of organization. While the traditional sole proprietorships are dominant in the western counties of central Iowa it is clear that corporate farms are heavily represented here. Figure 6.7 shows the distribution of the subtypes of corporations and LLCs – again the family corporations are present in the central part of the state but clearly non family corporations are responsible for much of the growth of swine production here. Thus the entry of non-family corporations into swine production in North Central Iowa seems to correlate well with a departure from the traditional pattern of swine production as an ecological adaptation by household producers. Whereas household producers raised hogs as a means of enhancing the income from poorer soils, the new corporate producers have chosen to locate near the large feed grain producing regions of the state.

How important are the corporate producers to the recent changes in Iowa's swine production? When the DNR data is combined with the ownership classification, other interesting patterns in the size of facilities emerge. Of the 400 entities that own the facilities, sole proprietorships outnumber corporations by more than 2:1. Yet when size and number of facilities are taken into account a different pattern emerges. Table 6.2 shows the breakdown of facilities by the form of business organization used by the owners. Although sole proprietor owned facilities outnumber corporate facilities, corporations still hold a strong lead in overall capacity.

Table 6.3 shows the same breakdown when the subtypes of corporations are considered. In this breakdown the non-family corporations still represent the largest segment of the entities in terms of capacity. However if the various forms of business organization used by families are taken into account, family owned corporations, LLCs, partnerships and sole proprietorships, family centered operations represent the largest class of producers both in the number of facilities and in capacity. Nonetheless, by this accounting, the growth in the number of swine production facilities owned by non-family based corporations represents a significant change for Iowa's swine industry. Table 6.4 lists the capacities of the 10 largest producers which together account for nearly 41% of the total liveweight capacity. Two firms, Decoster Farms of Iowa and Iowa Select Farms account for nearly 23% of the total liveweight capacity.

Contract Farming

In addition to forms of ownership or business organization, contract farming has also proliferated in Iowa's swine industry. Under a contract arrangement, farmers provide the facilities and labor to a contractor who in turn provides pigs and feed. Typically the farmer is paid a flat rate per finished animal with bonuses and penalties assigned for rate of gain and death loss as an incentive to managerial effort. Many farmers I met expressed skepticism about such arrangements, referring to the contract farmers as 'glorified hired men'. Others, particularly contract farmers themselves, regarded contract farming as one of the many options available to swine producers. Many saw contracting as a way for beginning farmers to enter an industry with increasingly high start up costs. Some farmers seemed envious of their contracting neighbors who erected sleek new facilities which contrasted with the older haphazardly constructed facilities on their own farms.

The firms contracting with farmers are some of the largest swine producers and feed companies in the industry. Iowa prohibits packers from owning feedlots or owning livestock under contract farming arrangements. This law, dating back to fears of the loss of family farmers and oligopolistic control of the nation's food supply, has resulted in a number of interesting permutations by corporations who skirt the intent of the law. One way they skirt the law is for farmers to take 'ownership' of pigs and be contractually bound to buying feed from the contractor and/or selling the pigs through marketing channels specified by the contractor. One of the largest of these contractors in Iowa is Murphy Farms of North Carolina.

Murphy Farms contracts with Iowa farmers to fatten pigs which are then sent to packing companies with which Murphy has production contracts. Due to the vast size of its operations Murphy can act as an effective conduit between the packers and numerous small farmers. Cargill, the world's largest agribusiness company, carries out much the same strategy by producing feeder pigs in other states then contracting the pigs to Iowa farmers for the final finishing stage before the fattened animals are shipped to Cargill owned Excel packing plants.

How does the ownership structure of the 588 new production facilities change when contract production is taken into account? Turning again to public records, I searched debts filed with the Iowa Secretary of State under the Uniform Commercial Code (UCC). All lenders in Iowa who obtain security interests for credit are required to file a notice of such interests with the Secretary of State listing the debtor, secured party, and a description of the collateral offered as security. For farmers such liens are routinely filed for the purchase of new machinery, livestock, or for operating lines of credit with local banks. Contract producers also file security agreements with the contractor when the latter finances pigs, feed, or the cost of new buildings and equipment.

I located all available UCC filings for the 400 firms and individuals identified as owners of the facilities in the DNR database. The result was 3573 individual filings dating from the 1960s to mid 1996. In chapter 7 I explore this data in greater detail for its implications concerning the institutional structure of agricultural credit. Here I note one particular aspect from this data that is crucial to understanding the ownership structure of Iowa's new swine facilities.

Above I noted that, despite the growing role of non-family swine production corporations in Iowa, family farm corporations and sole proprietorships still owned the greatest share of the newly constructed production capacity. If, however, the credit relationships of these farms are taken into account a much different picture emerges. By selecting those farms which have given security interests to non-family owned corporate swine producers, the actual amount of newly registered productive capacity under the *effective* control of family producers is drastically reduced. Viewed from this perspective, non-family corporate producers effectively control through contract production an additional 16.67% of overall production bringing their overall total to 54.59%. Family corporations and LLCs, partnerships, and sole proprietorships, all those entities that seem to embrace the traditional 'family farm' structure, account for only 35.12% of the total of this new production capacity.

This illustrates my point in chapter 2 concerning the difficulties of applying precise taxonomies to agricultural producers. When so many producers are, in the popular derisive term, corporate hired hands, ownership takes a back seat to indebtedness as a means of controlling productive assets. Family farms, family corporations, and contract producers all become rather hazy categories.

Farmers and Networks: Who Benefits?

A number of factors emerged in the 1990s to rekindle interest in cooperation among hog farmers. Many small towns and rural communities fear the effect of the loss of hog producers and the resulting dollars lost by such an exodus. Regional feed companies and cooperatives with ties to family farmers also fear the effect of dwindling numbers of hog producers. Others have a less direct stake. The leading national advocate for networks has been the National Pork Producers Council, with strong support from economists and livestock scientists at land grant universities (examples of their promotional efforts can be found in Dotson 1994, 1995). The very existence of these groups is questionable if their constituency disappears. In addition, veterinarians, bankers, and politicians have all supported networking. Many network organizers even report encouragement from packers who fear that dwindling numbers of producers will mean greater difficulty in obtaining hogs for slaughter.

The consensus from NPPC and land grant universities is that small producers must employ the approaches of the largest producers if they are to compete. The problem seems to lie in convincing a specific farmer to join forces with others. One would-be organizer pointed to the 'Community Nursery Handbook' developed by Iowa State's Team Pork and lamented, 'this tells me everything to do to get a network going, it just doesn't tell me how to convince the farmers to join.' In listening to organizers, extension workers, and farmers across Iowa, I heard a constant refrain - farmers are too independent, too much enamored of the go-it-alone philosophy of the yeoman to ever agree on anything much less cooperate with one another. That is the nature of the so-called 'people problem', the independence of the family farmer.

Contrary to stereotypes, independence never became much of an issue in the networks I studied. All, including the participants in both the failed and successful networks, were willing to go along so long as the usefulness or compatibility of the economic and technical aspects of the network fit the needs of their operation. It was not independence, not some stubborn ideology of going it alone, that caused the failure of Steve Longley's group but simply Longley's inability to identify a common need among the potential members and fit his network's goal to that need. The various interests that are promoting networks as an alternative for Iowa's rapidly industrializing swine industry frequently overlook the mundane realities of how cooperation between particular farms can come into existence. In the rush to organize and promote a solution that 'makes sense' from the perspective of the local feed mill or the offices of swine producers' associations and academics, many seem to overlook the fundamental need for tailoring solutions to the needs of individual farmers. That mistake reflects centralized mind-set that looks out on an economy and sees it operating under rules prescribed from above. Such visions can and have been carried out through the force of law and other means of coercion but very often fail due to some seemingly inexplicable internal collapse. As I mentioned earlier, the history of postwar anthropology is replete with examples of failed development schemes blamed on the backwardness and obstinacy of the locals. Far more promising and resilient are those economic arrangements that emerge when local decision making priorities are respected and local solutions are allowed to take shape.

Farmers and Cooperatives: A Short History

The notion that farmers can better themselves by cooperating with one another may be as old as farming itself. Anthropologists have described the communal nature of food production and distribution in a wide variety of cultures. The reciprocal sharing of labor in food production occurred among our hunter-gatherer ancestors and still occurs in peasant societies today. But the idea that farmers and other small producers in industrialized nation-states could gain economic clout by banding together has its origins in the cooperative movement of the 19th century.

In the 19th century, farmers in the United States formed various kinds of 'cooperative societies' to oppose centralized control from merchants, railroads, grain buyers, and packers. Operated as a form of collective bargaining, cooperatives attempted to curtail the market power of large firms by uniting the buying and selling of individuals under the collective clout of the cooperative. While one farmer may not have affected the price of wheat, ten thousand farmers agreeing to withhold their crops from the market could. Membership in cooperatives was limited to farmers themselves, to those who buy from or sell to the cooperative.

The decision making of the societies followed the principle of 'one member, one vote' rather than the one share, one vote practiced by corporations. In other words, no matter how much money he spent with the cooperative or how large his farm was, the voting power of the individual member was no greater than that of any other member. This form of economic democracy appealed to many and contributed to the success of cooperatives and their popular reputation for protecting the interests of the little guy (for a history of the cooperative movement see Rasmussen 1991).

Cooperatives attracted a strong following in many parts of the United States particularly among Northern European immigrants to the upper Midwest. Today cooperatives handle much of the interior movement of feed grains as well as significant quantities of farm supplies such as fertilizer and pesticides. Cooperatives in Iowa are chartered under a special section of the state's corporate law granting them special tax status and regulating the ownership of shares. The USDA and land grant universities maintain active programs to encourage the development of cooperatives. Many local cooperatives joined to form regional associations that count their sales in the hundreds of millions. These large cooperatives have become sophisticated businesses able to access capital and conduct trade on a national and international scale. Cooperative managers argue that they provide a force that brings economic benefits to their members that wouldn't exist if privately owned firms dominated agriculture. Critics of cooperatives argue that as cooperatives have grown in size and complexity they have lost their populist appeal and are now just another form of corporate agriculture (Hightower 1978, Kravitz 1974).

In the 1970s, farmers in Iowa began experimenting with cooperatives to produce feeder pigs, immature pigs weighing about 40 pounds, which were ready to be weaned from their mothers and started on a feeding program that would take them to market weight. The idea was to build a large centralized facility where the pigs would be born, known as a farrowing barn, hire a manager and employees to operate it, and distribute pigs to member farms for finishing. By the end of the 1970s over 80 such cooperatives existed in Iowa. These cooperatives were organized not as profit making businesses but to distribute feeder pigs to members at the cost of production (Paulsen and Rahm 1979). In addition members hoped to free themselves from labor intensive farrowing by shifting that activity to a specialist. By the 1990s few of these cooperatives remained or were operating with their original members. Many farmers described disagreements over management decisions and poor performance as reasons for the failure.

One area that large cooperatives have traditionally avoided is the actual production of agricultural commodities and livestock. Recent efforts by Farmland Industries, a large regional cooperative with its own packing operations, to fatten its own hogs by contracting with farmers has drawn sharp rebukes from the farm community (Des Moines Register 1994). Farmers I interviewed expressed resentment that an organization which they ostensibly own is also a competitor. Farmland, like other large cooperatives such as Land O' Lakes and Growmark, was reacting to the growth of large corporate swine operations that emerged in the late 1980s. Unlike the small family farmer who buys feed at his local cooperative, these integrated firms mill their own feed, bypassing either the cooperative or the privately owned feed company.

In an effort to stave off the economic consequences of such a shift, many in the feed industry and land grant universities have proposed networks as a new twist on the farmer cooperative. As used by social scientists a network represents the various ties of kinship, friendship, employment, patronage etc. between individuals. Network analysis forms a significant subdiscipline in anthropology and sociology. The term network had also been transformed into a verb (as in 'to network') by popular business writers who advocated networking as a means of strengthening businesses. In a sense, all cooperatives are networks, just as all businesses, schools, churches, and families are networks of ties and affiliations. The use of the term network by swine producers today carries many of these overtones but generally refers to the cooperative-like efforts of several farmers to establish some form of joint venture.

What distinguishes social networks as well as the early cooperatives is their grass roots nature. Perhaps the most important question facing many hog farmers today is whether they will direct the development of these new networks or whether they will confront approaches designed by others that are inappropriate to their needs. Will networks become merely another form of agribusiness cooperative more responsive to the goals of their hired managers than their farmer members? Many of the networks I described in chapter 4 face just this challenge.

Networks and Packers: Networking with Cargill

Another key question that I heard from many farmers was, can networks make a difference, can they make family producers sufficiently competitive with large-scale corporate producers? Many hog farmers express pessimism, they suspect that their own demise is inevitable. Although the use of networks to increase production efficiency and to reduce costs is rapidly proving itself to many farmers, the real benefit may lie in the ability to retain access to markets for their products. Already farmers and others note with worry the increasing ties between the largest swine producers and packers. These ties represent the kind of corporate networking that occurs in many industries. Ironically, the key question for the long term survival of family farms, indeed for many forms of household agricultural production, may be, is it possible to network with Cargill?

The experiences of Mary Vinton, described above, illustrate the possibilities for just this sort of arrangement. Where formerly several separate farms raised pigs and sold their finished animals to a packer, now one farm coordinates the activities of many farms through contractual arrangements. Each farm produces a component, a portion of the final product, by specializing in one phase of the swine growth cycle then shipping its pigs on to the next farm. It is these large central farms, coordinating the process, who are now linked into one larger group. The combined total production of this network of networks is some 80,000 finished hogs per year worth nearly $10,000,000. Their contract with Cargill's Excel Packing unit guarantees a minimum price over the course of one year. In their negotiations they pitted Cargill against the Midwest's largest packer IBP for access to a uniform and consistent supply of hogs. This strategy succeeded in part due to the efforts of Mary Vinton who, in addition to managing her family's own large farm, coordinates the network's activities. Because of her farm's active use of subcontractors as well as participation in two other information sharing networks this farmer entrepreneur occupies the same structural position as the Allan Garrison. In effect, she acts as a broker between the packers and other farmers. Rather than incurring numerous transaction costs in acquiring pigs directly from individual producers, the packer makes one transaction with the person occupying the structural position between itself and the network. Thus the network provides not only a benefit to its members but serves to minimize transaction costs for the packer as well.

A second attempt to use a network to gain an advantage with a packer is that made by Allan Garrison's Pig Palace proposal. During the time I worked with him, he and representatives from IBP, the nation's largest packer, met several times to discuss what steps would be necessary for IBP to kill and process hogs that could be identified with the farmers involved in the network. This effort is also described in greater detail in Chapter 4 above. Despite the apparent failure of the effort, what is important is the initial interest taken by IBP representatives in a small-scale project that might represent only a few days processing capacity at one IBP plant.

As large-scale producers take an increasing share of the market and at the same time commit their production to specific packers the competition for supplies among the remaining packers becomes more acute. Many in the swine industry described IBP as a hard nosed competitor that ten years ago would have laughed at the suggestion of contracting with a group of small farmers. Declines in available supplies of hogs may continue to create pressure on packers and farmers alike to look to networks for creative and mutually beneficial arrangements.

Farmers and the State

The transformation of hog farming has not occurred in the absence of state intervention. Hog farmers, like other producers, have encountered the state-sponsored strategies for the organization of agriculture embodied in former U.S. Agriculture Secretary Earl Butz's famous phrase 'get big or get out'. Neither that strategy nor the strategy of the government backed farmer cooperative movement, which might be termed 'get together and get big', has lived up to its promise.

Farm indebtedness, a result of 'getting big', increased dramatically in the expansive days of the 1970s, leading to massive defaults and record levels of federal aid to agriculture in the 1980s (Harl 1990). At the same time the cooperatives, which were for years the rallying cry of populism in the upper Midwest, have followed their own expansive strategies. The results have been similar with many local cooperatives being absorbed into larger regional organizations. Sales of these largest coops are measured in the billions of dollars (Freeman 1988). The result, despite the egalitarian image that still surrounds the idea of a cooperative, is that a coop's activities and presence in many communities is indistinguishable from that of any other agribusiness (Kravitz 1974). 'Farmer-owned' merely disguises the 'management-run' aspect of many coops. With the recent entry of coops into contract livestock production many farmers are (to paraphrase the old union rallying song) not so much 'stickin' with' but 'workin' for' the coop.

These issues are particularly relevant today as numerous family farmers in Iowa are encouraged to join swine production networks. Networks are being touted by government officials and land grant universities alike as a way for farmers to cooperatively improve the efficiency of their swine production operations - to once again get together and get big. The land grant universities, mindful of their own economic vulnerability, have mounted an eleventh hour effort to promote networking as a solution to the vulnerabilities of the independent farm. Unlike the founders of the original cooperative movement, with their confrontational stance toward 'big business', today's land grant academics encourage farmers to become big business. Extension workers advise farmers to formalize their networks as corporations with business plans and management teams. Even Allan Garrison remarked 'I'm gonna make businessmen out of them yet.'

Despite the dramatic decline in the number of farmers across the U.S., Iowa and other states continue to promote agricultural development strategies that encourage the kinds of high-risk expansions that have proven so disastrous for previous generations of farmers.

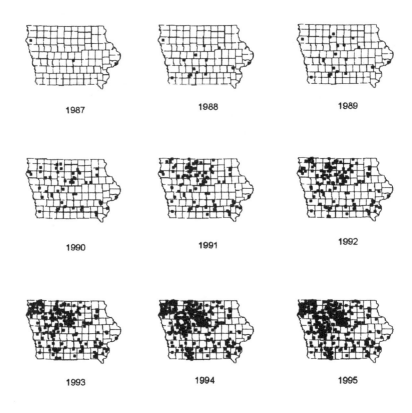

Figure 6.1 Cumulative growth in Iowa's registered swine facilities1987-1995 (Each dot represents 1 facility).

Table 6.1 Summary of swine facility construction activity in Iowa 1987-1995 (LW = liveweight capacity).

Year	Count of Facilities	Sum of LW	Avg. of LW	Min of LW	Max of LW
1987	3	279000.00	139500.00	119000.00	160000.00
1988	12	4774300.00	397858.33	49000.00	1759000.00
1989	6	1489000.00	248166.67	154000.00	450000.00
1990	37	14104470.00	391790.83	132500.00	1012500.00
1991	55	23431263.00	433912.28	91200.00	1620000.00
1992	55	27430347.00	498733.58	90000.00	1620000.00
1993	103	60363470.00	591798.73	84000.00	3780000.00
1994	168	125888977.00	753826.21	70000.00	2687000.00
1995	79	66362060.00	840026.08	120000.00	2310000.00
Pending	30	20890145.00	746076.61	210000.00	1960000.00
	548.00	345013032.00			

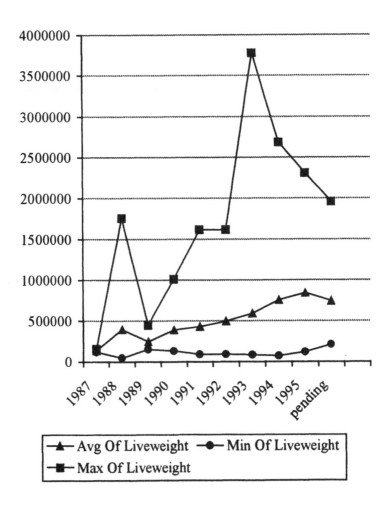

Figure 6.2 Changes in the size of the smallest, average, and largest facilities 1987-1995.

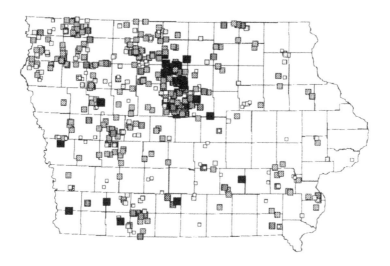

Size of facilities (lbs. liveweight capacity)
- □ 49000 - 264000
- ▫ 264000 - 435000
- ▨ 435000 - 904800
- ▨ 904800 - 1680000
- ■ 1680000 - 3780000
- ☐ County boundaries

Figure 6.3 Relative size of new swine facilities classed by liveweight capacity.

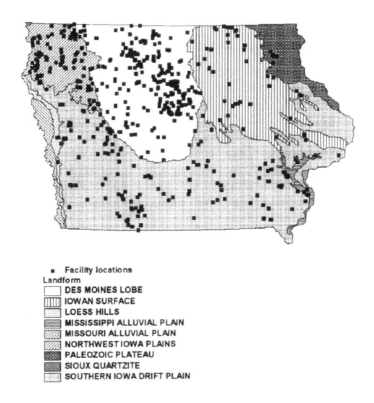

Figure 6.4 Location of new swine facilities in relation to major geologic regions of Iowa.

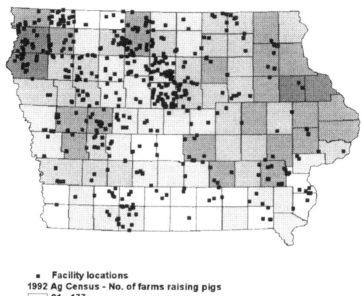

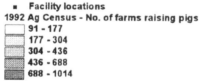

■ Facility locations
1992 Ag Census - No. of farms raising pigs
☐ 91 - 177
☐ 177 - 304
☐ 304 - 436
☐ 436 - 688
☐ 688 - 1014

Figure 6.5 Location of registered swine facilities in relation to other swine producing areas in Iowa.

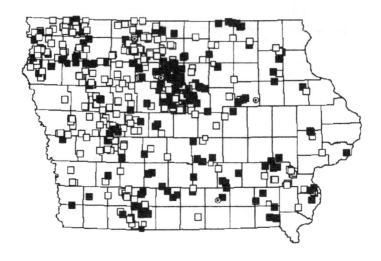

Form of business organization
- ■ Corporation
- ▪ LLC
- ▫ Partnership
- ▢ Sole Proprietor
- ◈ Uncertain
- ☐ County boundaries

Figure 6.6 Location and form of business organization of new swine facilities.

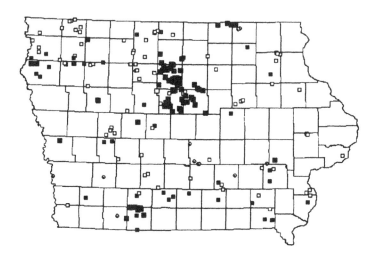

Form of business organization
- ■ Non Family Corp
- ■ Network
- ⊙ Uncertain
- ▫ Family corp.
- ▫ Cooperative
- ☐ County boundaries

Figure 6.7 Location of corporate owners of new swine facilities by type of corporation.

Table 6.2 Facility capacity by type of ownership (LW = liveweight capacity).

Entity type	Sum of LW	% of Total LW	Count of Facilities
CORPORATION	206989004.00	59.99%	225
SOLE PROPRIETOR	120707010.00	34.99%	288
PARTNERSHIP	8061600.00	2.34%	17
UNCERTAIN	4570485.00	1.32%	9
LLC	3346000.00	0.97%	5
PUBLIC	1030933.00	0.30%	3
TRUST	308000.00	0.09%	1
TOTAL	345013032.00	100.00%	548

Table 6.3 Facility capacity by type and subtype of ownership
(LW = liveweight capacity).

Entity type	Subtype	Sum of LW	% of LW	Count of facilities
CORPORATION	non family	130827301	37.92%	93
SOLE PROPRIETOR		120707010	34.99%	288
CORPORATION	family	41161853	11.93%	81
CORPORATION	network	27388550	7.94%	40
PARTNERSHIP		8061600	2.34%	17
CORPORATION	not determined	7279600	2.11%	10
UNCERTAIN		4570485	1.32%	9
LLC	not determined	1232000	0.36%	2
LLC	family	1124000	0.33%	2
PUBLIC		1030933	0.30%	3
LLC	network	990000	0.29%	1
CORPORATION	coop	331700	0.10%	1
TRUST		308000	0.09%	1
TOTAL		345013032		548

Table 6.4 Capacity of the 10 largest swine producers (LW = liveweight capacity, NFC = nonfamily corporation, NET = network).

Entity	Entity type	Sub-type	Sum of LW	No. of facilities	% of total LW
Decoster Farms of Iowa	Corp.	NFC	6046927 0	42	17.53%
Iowa Select Farms	Corp.	NFC	5233977 5	34	15.17%
Swine Graphics Enterprises LTD	Corp.	NET	5936700	6	1.72%
Trace Inc.	Corp.	NFC	5456256	5	1.58%
Conti-Feeders	Corp.	NFC	3780000	1	1.10%
Twin Pines Co.	Corp.	NET	2741200	2	0.79%
Rayle Tech Farm	Corp.	Fam.	2639820	4	0.77%
Anderson, Dallas	Sole Prop.		2557500	2	0.74%
Handlos, Lawrence F.	Sole Prop.		2520000	2	0.73%
Twin Valley Producers Network, Inc.	Corp.	NET	2128000	2	0.62%
					40.74%

7 A Model of Competition: The Structure of Credit in Iowa's Swine Industry

Introduction

In chapter 5 I introduced a model of cooperation that explains the ways in which farmers and network organizers form successful production networks. The purpose of that model was two-fold, first to address how cooperation comes about, and second, to provide a practical organizational tool for farmers and network organizers. In this chapter I address a quite different question but one, as I will show, that ultimately has a very similar answer. Before I asked about networks, how do they work and what makes them succeed? Here I ask, does it matter? Will cooperative networks have a competitive chance against other swine production strategies? Particularly, has networking provided farmers with greater financial strength and hence better access to credit markets? Does anything comparable to the micro-structure of the producer network exist in the macro-structure of the swine industry that would give small producers a competitive edge against the corporate producers? This effort attempts to use the model of cooperation as what Barth called a 'generative model'. In particular I ask if the social structural model of cooperation emphasizing the flow of information in a network as a key organizational variable can inform a broader social structural model of competition emphasizing credit relationships. Despite the obvious differences in the ends of cooperative and competitive behavior, I argue that the data presented below suggests such structural similarities between networks of cooperation and competition.

Barriers to entry in the swine industry are few. Access to capital is the chief limitation on how large swine producers can grow. In other words, there is no minimum size to swine production such as there is for automobile production. While a modern automotive plant requires an extensive facility to make a cost competitive product, a modern hog production facility can be quite small and achieve low per unit costs of production. Many hog producers enter the business by recycling existing farm structures. Similarly there are few technological hurdles to meet in order to enter swine production, no patented processes to hinder entry, and information on production methods and economics is widely available in the public domain. In order to enter swine production or to expand operations, farms require capital to construct facilities, to buy breeding or feeding stock, to purchase feed and other supplies, and to pay for the additional labor needed.

One thing that has traditionally limited many family-farming operations has been the availability of family labor. In recent years a number of large family based producers have expanded their operations by adding hired labor or contracting with neighboring producers. Although many household producers are content to operate at a scale consistent with available family labor, others have chosen expansive strategies in a search for greater profits. The last remaining barrier to entry and/or expansion for this latter group is the ability to access credit.

The supply of credit is a scarce resource like all other production inputs. Lenders seek to make loans to the most qualified borrowers. The largest corporate producers often obtain loans from large regional banks and in some cases from an international lender. One question facing networks as well as individual farmers is, can they compete for capital with these large-scale producers? At the same time agriculture itself doesn't exist in an economic vacuum. As a loan officer at one of the largest agricultural banks in Iowa explained to me, agricultural loans have not traditionally been as profitable as other forms of lending, for instance home mortgages. The competition, he felt, in the credit markets may be as likely to come from urban-based loans as from large-scale livestock production. As this lender phrased it, 'Would I rather make a house loan to a guy who works for the University of Iowa and has a stable monthly income or to a hog farmer?' Traditionally Iowa's small rural banks have not faced these choices. They lent money in the communities where they were based and those loans necessarily included farms.

Increasingly, however, Iowa banking is following a nationwide trend of bank consolidations with many small banks becoming part of large chains. Lending opportunities for these conglomerate banks are no longer limited to rural communities. The banker's comments also match those of farmers in the networks I studied. In Chapters 3 and 4 I noted many reports of the reluctance of local lenders to get involved in financing large scale facilities for networks.

The importance placed on credit is not a text book assumption but an observation that emerges from the ethnographic work described in

Chapters 3 and 4. While not all farmers or all networks have chosen an operational goal that requires extensive credit, many have. Most of the dozen groups I met with were involved in trying to obtain financing for their network venture. In this chapter I describe the origins of the financial information needed for credit applications and, in many cases, the dubious value of this information for networks. I then use a 'trace measurement' by tracking the credit histories of the 400 swine producers discussed in Chapter 6. The purpose of this phase of the research is to link the micro-social structure of network organizations to the macro-social structure of the swine industry. I look at whether credit relationships, as 'gateway' indicators of competitive strength, differ between various kinds of producers. In particular, do non-family corporate swine producers and contract producers have patterns of credit relationships that might account for their dominant share of new capacity as described in Chapter 6? If so, is there any indication that networks have a comparable ability to access credit that would allow them to compete with the largest producers?

Classifying Creditor/Borrower Characteristics

In order to assess how changes in the swine industry and in banking have affected Iowa farmers I return to the database of hog facilities taken from Iowa Department of Natural Resources records. Recall that these are mostly large scale facilities with open manure lagoons, which are required by state law to obtain a permit and are a source of controversy.

From the list of facilities, I identified 400 entities as owners and classified these owners according to the form of business organization they used. I further classified corporations as family, non-family, or network, based on records of owners and officers filed with the Iowa Secretary of State. I then collected records of security interests that the various entities had given in order to obtain credit. Once these records were collected I identified the lenders and categorized the records as shown in the tables located at the end of this chapter. I was able to obtain further information on many individual banks using an Iowa bank directory (Sheshunoff 1996). I then assigned a code to each bank loan identifying the particular institution. Many of the banks listed in the Secretary of State's records were no longer in existence or had been acquired by other banks. All of these banks were assigned to their successors. The result is a comprehensive database of lending relationships between the 400 entities that have built new facilities in recent years and the banks and other companies that finance those entities.

The resulting database of credit relationships contains 3572 records of security interest filings. The records consist of initial filings, amendments, continuations, partial releases, and terminations. The records cover the period from 1965 through July, 1996. Below I examine these records for patterns in the lending relationships that might provide some insight on the ability of family farmers and networks to compete with large corporate producers. As I argued above, access to credit is an important key to competitive success. What I'm looking for here are differences in the patterns of credit access between the large corporate producers and the household producers or the networks of household producers. First I describe what kinds of producers obtain money from what kinds of lenders. I classify producers according to their form of business organization as well as the size of facilities they have constructed. I classify lenders according to the type of firm. For banks I also use classifications based on the size of the bank and on the amount of agricultural lending the bank is involved in. Finally I look at patterns in the lending relationships themselves.

From January, 1986 through July, 1996 (the period during which the permitted facilities were constructed) there were 1813 initial filings of security interests. Table 7.1 shows the number of filings by various types of lenders in total and to the different types of swine producers (tables follow page 121). Banks, machinery dealers and swine production companies were the most active in terms of the total number of loans made. It should be noted that some of the loans involved may be unrelated to swine production. Loans to machinery dealers appear to be primarily to the major farm equipment companies who produce machines primarily for field crop production. Likewise loans to the Farm Service Agency/Commodity Credit Corporation are secured by a farmer's crops and may not be directly related to swine production. However the presence of loans to these two types of lenders suggests that the borrower is involved in crop farming, a fact which distinguishes many of the smaller producers. Farm Credit Services, the farmer owned lending cooperative, also recorded substantial filings to corporations as well as sole proprietors. Notably the swine production companies record proportionally fewer loans to other corporations than to sole proprietors. Table 7.2 shows the breakdown of filings by the various types of corporations. Here too the pattern of predominantly bank lending continues, especially for networks. At the same time several other lenders make proportionally more loans to family farm corporations than to other types of corporations. Farm Credit Services and regional feed companies are notable for the number of loans made to family corporations. Table 7.3 divides producers into quartiles based on the total liveweight capacity of facilities owned by each entity. Although many categories of lenders, including banks, are fairly evenly spread across the range of producer sizes, swine production companies and Farm Credit Services are noticeably underrepresented in the first quartile of producers ranked by size of facilities.

Tables 7.4 – 7.9 look at the characteristics of bank loans, repeating the classification scheme for swine producers used in the previous tables. Of the 504 initial filings by banks in 444 loans could be identified with Iowa based banks. Tables 7.4 – 7.6 count the number of filings by banks in each of four quartiles of total bank assets. Correlations were calculated for all of the relationships. In calculating correlations I used the actual size for each entity rather than quartile rank. I also ran correlations for all of the filings controlling for entities with multiple filings with one lender. No significant overall correlations were obtained between bank size and facility size of the borrowers ($r=.0242$ n.s.). It is worth noting that the largest banks did file far more security agreements than the smallest banks for all classes of producers.

Tables 7.7 – 7.9 repeat the analysis of the previous tables, this time classifying banks according to the size of their outstanding agricultural loan portfolio. Again larger banks make more loans but no significant correlations existed in the overall relationship between agricultural loan portfolio size and the size of swine facilities ($r=.0248$ n.s.). I also ran crosstabulations based on the percentage of the bank's loan portfolio in agricultural loans. These tables, not shown here, also showed lending to be evenly distributed between all classes of borrowers and lenders.

On the surface at least these tables seem to imply that credit is widely available from a variety of sources. Small farms, sole proprietors and networks all seem to be borrowing from the same variety of lenders as large farms and non-family corporations. One possible exception seems to be that the smallest farms are not as well connected to swine production companies or the Farm Credit Service. Networks seem to rely primarily on bank lending but a variety of other capital sources are in use.

Does this mean that networks and family farms enjoy a competitive position in their ability to acquire credit? Perhaps. On the other hand, one troubling aspect of this analysis is that the swine production companies have a very high number of loans among sole proprietorships, particularly in the top three quartiles. Most of the classes of lenders identified in the tables either loan money to farmers to purchase production supplies (e.g. bank loans) or to finance purchases of products from the lender itself (e.g. feed company loans). Swine production companies are an exception because of the nature of the contract feeding arrangement. Whereas the farmer borrowing from his local bank or coop retains a certain degree of autonomy as a producer, the contract farmer gives up much of that autonomy in exchange for the supposed benefits of the contract. Recall that when contract producers were counted with non-family corporate producers the combined group controlled the majority of the capacity of new production facilities. As I argued in Chapter 2 the relevance of classification schemes begins to break down once we begin to consider all of the relationships that exist in the economy. Should the contract producers be counted as medium scale family farms or should they be considered part of the corporate farming structure? For the purposes of analyzing the swine industry they really are in the latter category. But it doesn't matter what we call them. The simple fact that over 50% of new production capacity is in the effective control of the corporate producers is the most significant finding.

In a credit environment where funds are seemingly available from a wide variety of lenders what explains the dominance of the corporate producers? In particular, when the actual ownership records and debt filings are examined it appears that nearly half of all the new productive capacity is in the hands of just three firms – Decoster Farms, Iowa Select Farms, and Murphy Farms. In the next section I offer a possible explanation for the current structure of the swine industry in Iowa. I then suggest a model for competition that ties in with the model of cooperation developed in the previous chapter.

The Structure of Credit Networks

How do the largest producers come to dominate an industry and how can farmers or networks of farmers compete with this dominance? In the cases of Decoster Farms and Iowa Select Farms the credit ties that allow these firms to finance their expansion are fairly straightforward. Decoster Farms is financed by insurer Metropolitan Life and by one of the world's largest agricultural lenders, Netherlands based Rabobank. Rabobank has recently expanded its agricultural lending in the United States. Rabobank spokespersons and numerous industry analysts credit the bank's lending successes to its detailed knowledge of the markets where it operates. Very often Rabobank finances both sides of a trading relationship or many players in an industry, giving the bank an edge in understanding critical performance characteristics of firms. In the swine industry Rabobank loans money not only to Decoster, but to Murphy Family Farms, North Carolina based packer Smithfield Foods, and Missouri's Premium Standard Farms (Perkins 1995, Bronstein 1996). Similarly, Iowa Select Farms, though much smaller than Decoster, arranges financing through a large regional lender, Denver based FBS Ag Credit the agricultural lending arm of Minneapolis based FirstBank. Iowa Select also receives financing from the Farm Credit System and several smaller Iowa lenders. The ability to access credit on a regional and international scale through lenders whose ties extend not downward into small farm communities but upward into packing and food processing, is crucial to the largest producers such as Decoster, Murphy, and Iowa Select. However, such relationships are often lost in a taxonomic analysis.

The case of Murphy Farms and its ties to numerous family producers in Iowa is a somewhat more complicated matter. One argument for the type of production strategy pursued by Decoster and Iowa Select is the classical transaction cost approach. A firm produces its goods in house when the transaction cost of obtaining those goods in the market exceeds the in house cost. It is simply a more efficient production strategy for Decoster and Iowa Select, like other large producers, to control the swine production process from start to finish. These companies enjoy economies of transacting and pass along such economies to the packers who need only deal with a few large suppliers rather than numerous small ones (see Barkema and Cook 1993 for an interesting review of this possibility by two Federal Reserve Bank economists).

What then explains Murphy's rise to prominence as the nation's largest swine producer? What advantage does Murphy gain as a contractor with numerous producers rather than becoming a vertically integrated producer? Arguably one advantage for Murphy is to shift risk and cost onto the shoulders of its contractors, a strategy employed in the poultry industry (Lee 1996). Internally, managerial demands are less than in a tightly integrated firm. At the same time it would seem such savings could be lost in the cost of transacting with the numerous contractors.

Table 7.10 below summarizes initial filings made by those farms which have at least one security agreement with Murphy Farms. Of particular interest is the pattern that emerges between the many loans made by Murphy Farms and those made by other types of creditors. Whereas Table 7.4 showed that the 400 entities in this database gave the most security interests to banks, Table 7.10 shows that Murphy's contract farmers file most frequently with Murphy. This suggests that Murphy's contract producers depend on Murphy's financial assistance to a greater degree than the other producers in the database. Of the 78 producers giving security interests to Murphy, 12 show no record of loans to any other lender.

Murphy loans to two distinct groups. In one group are producers and lenders who have multiple connections. This pattern suggests borrowers and lenders who have a wide range of choices in credit transactions. In the second group are producers who are linked to no other lenders or to only one lender. This pattern suggests lenders and borrowers who are relatively isolated in terms of other participants in Murphy's contract production scheme. There are 34 producers in the first group and 44 producers in the second. Inasmuch as banks may act as conduits for information between borrowers, the relative isolation of the borrowers in the second may explain part of Murphy's success. Being a principal source of credit to producers with few other lending options may enhance Murphy's ability to arrange the terms of contracts to its favor. In other words producers with a fewer ties to lenders may be less likely to bargain for better contract terms than producers with more ties. At the same time the more densely connected group may provide advantages to Murphy as well. Here the overlapping ties of other lenders may serve to provide an information network to Murphy which reduces the effort needed in identifying new contract producers. The banks may, in effect, act as filters for Murphy.

In an industry where capital is a crucial barrier to entry and expansion, access to regional and international sources of credit and the creation of a network of contract producers appears to provide an explanation for Murphy's rise to the top. Murphy's network appears to be a strategic adaptation to the credit market. How then do the networks identified in the DNR database fare compared to Murphy and its contract producers? Table 7.2 showed that networks were primarily bank financed. Some networks have access to 2 or more lenders. At the same time some lenders are focal point for lending to several networks. Overall however the pattern for the networks is relatively disconnected. Many networks are relatively isolated, connected to only one source of credit. At the same time, that credit source is isolated as well, at least in terms of lending to networks. The contrast with Murphy's network is quite clear. Murphy is financed by a variety of large lenders. Murphy is a lender as well, acting as a focal point for two very different groups of contract producers. All three types of credit network may serve Murphy's advantage. Externally, Murphy taps into the same sources of credit, such as Rabobank, as the other large swine production companies. Internally Murphy mimics the role of a centralized lender like Rabobank through two very different contracting networks. One network may provide relative ease in bargaining, the other relative ease in collecting information about potential contractors. In contrast, producer networks are, like Murphy's contractors, isolated from one another. At least in terms of access to credit, networking appears to be localized when compared to an extensive pattern such as Murphy Farms. It may be that, to be competitive with Murphy and the other large producers, the producer networks need to form a 'network of networks'.

Toward a Model of Competition

In the case of competitive success in the swine industry, several factors need to be weighed before coming to understand the competitive advantage enjoyed by the large firms. Economists might argue that these firms succeed because they are more efficient, i.e. better managers, better at controlling costs, better marketers. Yet that explanation ignores the fact that many small farmers reportedly have lower costs of production than the capital intensive mega-farms. If efficiency were a sufficient explanation for success in swine production then why are these efficient small farmers leaving the industry? An alternative explanation is that the large producers may manipulate the political process so as to gain special treatment under the law that provides them with a competitive advantage.

Travelling through North Carolina I heard many residents refer to 'Murphy's law', a package of legislation enacted while Murphy Farms' president Wendell Murphy was a member of the state legislature. Murphy helped write the rules of the game so as to insulate his activities from nuisance suits and gain an edge on North Carolina's swine industry. This political explanation, to which I will return in the last chapter, may be a necessary precondition for the success of firms like Murphy Farms, but it too lacks a sufficient explanation of how those rewritten rules are implemented. In other words, Wendell Murphy may have written the rules but we still need to know how he plays the game.

The explanation I propose for competitive success extends the explanation proposed for cooperative success in the previous chapter. Recall that one of the ways the organizer of a network succeeded was through the ability to identify and link compatible farms. The network organizer is first a conduit for information and second a catalyst for action. In the same fashion this network concept may explain the success of a firm like Murphy Farms. Just as Allan Garrison linked a group of strangers into a purposeful network so too Murphy Farms links a diverse body of lending institutions and farmers into its own sort of network. Coupled with the clout Murphy Farms enjoys through its manipulation of the political process, as well as its sheer size in the market, this networked 'farm' acts as a conduit and catalyst in the same way as the small scale network organizer. Easton, discussing industrial networks, offers this explanation of a firm's rationale for entering into networking relationships (1992:9):

> A relationship implies a measure of control over another organisation and, through that organisation, the environment. The consequent reduction in uncertainty and increase in stability may be very valuable objectives for many organizations. Similarly a relationship offers access to third parties who may have resources that are either valuable or essential to survival. One such resource is information and relationships can serve as data conduits and provide firms with a perspective on what is taking place in distant parts of the network.

This connectedness may well explain Murphy's success when compared to the recent financial debacle faced by the highly centralized, vertically integrated Premium Standard Farms (Jereski and Smith 1996). This arrangement also makes Murphy's operation less visible. The difference between an Allan Garrison and a Wendell Murphy is great when measured in terms of sheer scale and economic power, but in terms of their ability to navigate the social structure of cooperation and competition both utilize their positional advantages to achieve the ends they seek. The alternatives to of these strategies have proven far less successful.

The use of credit as a regulator of entry and expansion in the swine industry is similar to the role of a network organizer as a regulator of information in a network of farmers. How that regulatory function is used depends on the purposes to be achieved. Murphy Farms, in its drive for profit, appears to be in a position to use credit, as both borrower and lender, in order to further its profit motive. Allan Garrison, in attempting to provide benefits to his customers, is in the position to use information to further his and their goals. In that sense competition and cooperation are not so far apart as they might seem. Even though they produce very different outcomes, Murphy and Garrison employ similar techniques in managing the social structure of competition and cooperation. What unites them is their ability to use their structural positions to manipulate the flow of information and/or credit to their advantage. Burt's analysis of competitiveness as enhanced by the structural 'hole' seems to apply equally to Murphy and to the efforts of network organizers (1992:190):

> Competition is not about being a player with certain physical attributes; it is about securing productive relationships. Physical attributes are a correlate, not a cause, of competitive success. [Structural] Holes can have different effects for people with different attributes or for organizations of different kinds, but that is because the attributes and organization forms are correlated with different positions in the social structure. The manner in which a structural hole is an entrepreneurial opportunity for information and control benefits is the bedrock explanation that carries across player attributes, populations, and time.

Farmers and network organizers looking for ways to survive the changes occurring in the swine industry are faced with two challenges. First they must learn to work within the social structure of their local communities, managing the flow of information to achieve compatible networks of farms. Some of the networks described above have achieved that level of cooperation. At the same time, once these local networks have overcome their organizational and operational hurdles, they must face the task of meeting the competitive challenges of the industry - particularly the ability to access credit for entry and expansion. From the evidence presented here it appears that the farmer networks have not achieved the same level of success in integrating their networks with the credit markets as that achieved by the nation's largest producer, Murphy Farms. The biggest challenge for the producer networks may be to build the kinds of interlocking credit connections that Murphy has created. In the same way that Murphy maintains an effective network of producers by acting as the regulator of credit, so too farmer networks may need to look for ways to merge and regulate their own credit requirements.

The answer does not lie in piling on more and more dollars, the answer lies in constructing relationships with a wide variety of participants in order to enhance one's competitive position (cf. Burt 1992). Producer networks are relatively isolated in this regard compared to the extensive connections enjoyed by Murphy Farms. However, instead of fostering the kinds of interconnections between various networks and bankers across Iowa that could form a competitive 'network of networks', the land grant university academics who advise networks have retained a parochial emphasis on the production and growth strategies of individual networks. The potential consequences of this advice is discussed in the following section. I argue that rather than encourage the broad alliances that might give producer networks real competitive strength in the industry, these advisers are promoting large-scale projects built on dubious financial projections.

Networks and Bankers: The Rise of the Spreadsheet Farm

In this section, I look at some of the experiences of farmers and lenders in attempting to build financial projections for networks. The structural picture that emerges suggests an 'information gap' between farmers and lenders based on differences in the accounting used by each. It is, as I noted in chapter 2, a case where the standards of estimability vary (Douglas 1992). So too is there an information gap between the financial projections of networks and the expectations of lenders.

Tim Ingold has written that anthropologists frequently challenge accounts of the world produced in academia (1996:1):

> along with the implicit ranking of such accounts above those that
> might be offered by 'ordinary folk' whose powers of observation
> and reason have supposedly not been cultivated to the same
> degree.

Of the many types of accounts of the world, attempts to describe and forecast the operation of a farm are as varied as the tellers of the tale. Many of the widely accepted standards of financial accounting that prevail in the business world are little used in farming communities. At the same time many farmers have accumulated substantial assets with little more than a sharp pencil and a pocket notebook in which to do the simple arithmetic of gain. In this section I discuss the ways in which academics and lenders have attempted to revise household producer's accounts of their financial world in order to move agriculture into the wider frame of commercial business and credit markets.

As everyone from small town merchants to academics and industry leaders attempted to get on the bandwagon of farmer networks, a key question remained unanswered – would the bankers back such arrangements? One of the interesting aspects of swine production is the limitation that credit puts on entry to the industry. Unlike other industries, where specialized technical knowledge, trade secrets, or economies of scale often restrict would be entrants, swine producers have traditionally been limited only by the availability of capital. As interest in networks grew, one of the first problems to be solved was how to organize the network itself and how to plan and communicate its financial strategy. Here I explore the increasing use of computer-based financial projections of hog production, how those projections contrast with the mental accounting used by farmers, and how they have been adopted by the promoters of networks. I argue that in their attempt to transform untidy household production along the lines of the 'business model' of agriculture, land grant academics, extension advisers, and bankers are operating with information of dubious value.

As the popularity and affordability of personal computers increased in the mid-1980s, many farmers turned to the computer as an aid in dealing with increasingly complex financial issues in farming. Computer software specifically tailored for various kinds of farming activities appeared from Iowa State and other land grant universities. Farmers, bankers, and Extension Service workers embraced computer aided solutions to a number of production and financial problems. These programs can be divided into three types according to their intended use – 1) production record keeping, 2) accounting, and 3) budgeting and forecasting.

Many of these programs were written as 'templates' for an underlying application program such as the popular spreadsheet Lotus 123. The spreadsheet became an important tool in the creation of financial models and projections because of its ease of use and adaptability. Farmers and their bankers soon were able to play various 'what if' scenarios, using simplified models of farming activities built around the spreadsheet interface.

Hog farmers have been the target of a number of computer based innovations in record keeping and modeling. Extension advisers and farm journalists frequently lament the number of hog farms where production record keeping is nonexistent or minimal (much as Miner noted 50 years ago). Increasingly banks require record keeping systems that go far beyond the cash basis bookkeeping traditionally done on many farms. Yet despite the sophistication of the software available and the well-intentioned advice of many in the agricultural community, the extent to which farmers have made use of these new products is somewhat uncertain. One of the problems with computer aided solutions to farm production is the need for precise data on which to base projections. Despite the availability of many types of measuring and record keeping products, many farms I encountered failed to employ these technologies. In effect, farmers' 'accounts' of the world often fall short of the accounts they are required to give to make adequate use of the new information processing technologies.

In the field, I encountered many hog farmers who kept few records beyond what was minimally necessary for reporting to the Internal Revenue Service. Many others kept records only to the extent that they could be maintained with little effort. I learned to identify the various levels of record keeping present on a farm. The presence of 'sow cards' in the farm's farrowing house was generally the first level of record keeping. A sow card is simply a record of an individual animal's breeding history – the number of farrowings, number of live pigs weaned, and health. Farmers who use such simple records generally attach them to a small clipboard and hang them above the pen where the animal is kept. On some farms these are handwritten, on others they are computer printouts. The computerized records are often kept not by the farmer but by the farm's feed supplier or veterinary clinic who provide such services as a way of adding value to their own products. Without this type of record it becomes impossible to know how many litters a sow has had or to identify animals with low productivity.

A step up from the sow card is the presence of some sort of weighing device. Livestock production is after all a matter of increasing the weight of animals. Surprisingly even the simplest of scales were rarely present on the farms I visited. The veterinarian I accompanied often expressed his consternation at this situation, so much so that he carried a line of livestock scales as one of the products, along with vaccines and drugs, that he offered to clients. The veterinarian argued that without weighing even a sample of animals at different phases in their growth process little can be known about such things as feed efficiency or the effectiveness of various feed supplements.

All of the farmers I met expressed similar sentiments about the need for better record keeping. Several seemed clearly apologetic about their own shortcomings in this regard. Having been lectured and cajoled by their extension advisers and veterinarians, as well as in the pages of the ubiquitous farming magazines, all of these farmers were clearly aware of the need to improve their record keeping. Many talked of the importance of buying a personal computer in order to make the process of tracking their production and financial records simpler. The fact that so few of these intentions ever seemed to materialize into a concrete program appeared to reflect two underlying causes.

First, most of the farmers I encountered were not just hog farmers but often raised one other class of livestock (typically cattle), as well as crops of corn and soybeans. Many held off-farm jobs. Using little hired labor, they were occupied with all of the chores that go with running a farm, leaving little time for measuring and recording. Second, and perhaps more important, is the tradition of 'the farmer's eye'. By that I mean the ability of the individual farmer as a judge of the performance of crops and livestock based on frequent observation. A farmer with a good eye doesn't need to be told the rate of gain of a pen of pigs, he knows by looking at them that 'they're growin' good'. This is not just a matter of an economy of effort, but of pride in one's skill as a farmer. Like the supposed skill of a fishing boat captain in getting a large catch, the success of the farmer is based on the ability to judge without recourse to precise measurement (cf. Palsson and Durrenberger 1993). It is a crucial part of his or her account of the world that that world can be understood at an experiential level.

This reliance on skill often frustrates those whose own efforts are supposedly based on something more measurable, particularly bankers. Agricultural bankers have embraced many of the new software tools for analyzing the performance and evaluating the projections of their farmer customers. The use of spreadsheets for playing what-if games has lessened the burden of hand calculation for budgeting and cash flow analysis. It has also changed the nature of farm lending from a personal relationship between lender and borrower where reputations were often more solid than balance sheets to one of impersonal calculation. It's not that reputation and experience are ignored in the current lending climate, but rather that those attributes are coupled with a greater reliance on a standardized set of expectations concerning financial records and projections.

As I talked with farmers and bankers involved in creating new swine production networks, I encountered two problems with what I call 'spreadsheet farms'. Both of these issues are related to the traditional concerns of anthropologists with models and with the concept of transaction cost as introduced by the New Institutional Economics. The first issue concerns the gap between the precise calculations of a spreadsheet model and the less refined calculations of the farmer. Iowa State University has developed a spreadsheet template known as PigFlow. The purpose of PigFlow is to assist a farmer in determining how many pigs he has available in various stages of production in order to maximize his facilities. I've seen this program used on laptop computers by Extension workers, vets, feed salesman, and breeders alike as they attempt to persuade a farmer to adopt some sort of innovation. These demonstrations frequently make very persuasive cases for the benefits of a new technology or husbandry practice. The problem is that several key categories require the kind of measuring and recording that is lacking on most farms. As a result, not only are the inputs simply guesses, but assuming the farmer adopts the recommended practice, so too are the results. In other words, the spreadsheet exists independently of the underlying reality with little or no opportunity for verification either of its inputs or the results of adopting a proposed innovation. In many cases I observed farmers merely guessing at answers in order to fill in the blanks of the spreadsheet. This gap between the kinds of measurements made by farmers and those required by a spreadsheet illustrates the problems of using categories with dubious empirical footing. It's not that farmers can't determine such things as rate of gain when evaluating, for instance, a salesman's claims about a new feed additive. Rather, the costs of such a determination are too high since too much time must be devoted to verifying the performance of the new product relative to all of the other demands on the farmer's time. Additionally, such measuring often violates a set of cultural assumptions or rules about what constitutes a good hog farmer. As one farmer put it when I asked him why he didn't make all of these measurements – 'It's a lot of fuckin' around when I can just look at them pigs and tell how they're doin''.

The real benefit of computerized financial projections then seems to accrue to those who are pushing their particular innovation on the farmer. Not only is the input data a mish mash of guesses but given a similar inability to assess results in any but the most rudimentary terms, i.e. did I make money this year or not? so too are the results. Thus the supposed sophistication of the computer and the spreadsheet belies their use as slick peddler's tools.

Lest this seem like an analysis of how yet again the unassuming farmer is duped by the clever salesman I want to explore the second problem with spreadsheet models. In the example of PigFlow above, in all fairness to many of the cases in which I've seen the program used, there has been some underlying research to justify the input values chosen. Generally university or private researchers have conducted precise trials of a new product or practice which provide some justification for the assumptions involved. Clearly this may be of little comfort to a farmer who adopts such innovations not knowing if his own starting point in any way corresponds to the assumptions. Yet as tenuous as this hold on reality may seem, other spreadsheet models are taking the what-if scenarios even further.

I was given a spreadsheet by a 63 year-old farmer that depicted a cash flow projection for a 1200 sow farrowing unit that a regional feed company was proposing to build on a corner of the farmer's property. The farmer and several of his neighbors would be investors in this project which would be managed by and obtain its feed from the feed company. The farmer told me he had been assured a 30% return which is why he was willing to contribute the land for this facility as part of his investment. The spreadsheet page was but one of an inch thick packet of such projections the farmer showed me. A few calculations showed that the 30% return he expected to receive wouldn't materialize until year 10, the overall return is closer to 8%. But the even more interesting aspect of the projection was that in order to achieve such a return it held all factors constant over the 10 year planning period. In other words the assumptions of this model are that labor, feed, veterinary services etc., will cost no more 10 years from now than they do today and that the price of hogs will remain constant as well. While this may seem a strikingly naïve way to plan a multimillion dollar business investment, it is all too common among the groups I met who were planning similar projects. Both Steve Longley's group and the veterinarians in Harrisburg relied on similar spreadsheets.

Many of these projections also originated from the Extension advisers at Iowa State. At the simplest level, it reflects the way in which the mechanical process of spreadsheet creation can masquerade as a financial projection. Merely copying formulas from one column of cells to another gives an illusion of certitude, of profits advancing reliably into the future. Printed out on expensive paper and pitched by erstwhile Ag School graduates these plans carry an assurance of reliability and certitude. At another level these projections reflect a strange degree of self-deception on the part of their proponents as well. Typically these spreadsheets are presented to a group of farmers by a cooperative or a feed company seeking to enroll the farmers in a swine production network. Not having collected the data on their own farms with which they could test these assumptions, the farmers often have little ability to evaluate the projections. But they are also part of the financial planning package eventually used by these farmers when they approach lenders. In reality it is the lenders for whom such plans are constructed in the first place. One of the large regional cooperatives involved in promoting swine production networks employs a rural sociologist as a financing specialist whose job it is to present the details of these projections to lenders on behalf of a network of local farmers. Like the simple assumptions of the PigFlow program, the assumptions of these spreadsheet cash flow projections are equally lacking any empirical basis. While a feed company may have numerous trials to back up its PigFlow claims, the promoters of new swine production ventures often have little more than guesses on paper.

In all of this, the farmers themselves are passive participants since for most the scale and complexity of the new facilities exceeds anything on their own farms. The farmers and their bankers alike are in effect going along with the story presented in the spreadsheet – a story that may be based more on the credibility of the teller than of the tale itself. That the future will resemble the past is an assumption as easily made as copying spreadsheet columns from left to right.

That the lending community has become a willing participant in these spreadsheet farms should be no surprise to anyone with a memory of agricultural lending practices in Iowa over the last twenty years (for those who don't see Harl 1990). In the 1970s the equivalent assumption being made was that land prices would continue their double-digit annual increases and that operating losses could merely be refinanced by the increasing equity in land. The massive farm bankruptcies, bank failures, and near collapse of the Farm Credit System in the early 1980s, testify to the degree to which simple assumptions can inflame the madness of a crowd. The spreadsheet farm has now replaced the ever-appreciating farm as the pot at the end of the rainbow. The certainty on the part of land grant university academics and lenders alike that the small independent family farm is doomed has led to the wishful thinking exhibited by these spreadsheet farms. In place of the untidiness of the household operation mired in its traditional inefficiencies the spreadsheet farm promises professional management, a competitive future, and predictable returns. Thus the lending community embraces these projections more as the justification for its assumptions than on any basis of experience. It is an accepted fact that small farms cannot compete with corporate farms. When presented with farmer originated alternatives to these capital-intensive projects, many lenders have been quick to dismiss them as unrealistic. The solution proposed by so many of these spreadsheet farms is to in effect transform the family farms into corporate farms while preserving the lending and sales bases of local bankers and merchants.

What the spreadsheet farm does for bankers can be understood in terms of the transaction cost framework. Inasmuch as the record keeping on hog farms has traditionally been minimal, this new enterprise offers the lender the opportunity to reduce the cost of monitoring performance. In place of 10 decision makers each with their own plans, managerial skills, and financial peculiarities, the spreadsheet farm offers a single 'package', centralized management, and standardized projections and financial reports. All in all, it simply appears cheaper and safer for the bank to make a single one million-dollar loan than ten one hundred thousand dollar loans – especially if the same ten farmers agree to guarantee the million-dollar loan. Given the substantial amount of guesswork present in these 'spreadsheet farms' it is not just farmers who are being duped, but the supposedly careful, calculating lenders.

If there are any number of victims to be found in this fool's paradise of cooked books and guesses, who are the villains? It may be less a matter of villainy than the emergent properties of the complex relationships that exist between various banks, corporate swine producers, packers, and large cooperatives.

However, instead of aiding farmers in building the kinds of broad networks of relationships that would mimic the network used by Murphy and other large producers, the land grant universities are content to pursue their dreams of spreadsheet farms. The presence of unrealistic models reflects the wishful thinking of any number of players in Iowa's swine industry. Agriculture, it is argued, belongs to the bean counters and modelers who purport to see the future with their spreadsheets. The problem is that that vision of the future may have more to do with the desires of certain economic and political interests than any projection based on solid evidence.

Attempts to write the rules of the game should not be confused with attempts to understand the rules themselves. The contribution that anthropology makes in this situation is to challenge models that promote the economic and political interests of a few rather than a set of scientific generalizations useful for all.

Table 7.1 Initial filings by type of lender and type of producer.

Lender type	Total	Corp	LL	Ptr.	Pub.	Sole	Trust
Banks	504	140	4	27	3	330	
Machinery	382	113		30	1	238	
Swine Production Company	216	19	2	7		187	1
Farm Services Admin.	212	42		9		161	
Farm Credit Services	125	57	1	6		61	
Cooperative - Regional	69	25		4		40	
Grain/ Feed Company	62	48	1			13	
Individuals	41	9		3		29	
Leasing Company	33	15			2	16	
Finance Company - Non Bank	32	6		1		25	
Cooperatives - Local	26	2		2		22	
Uncertain/Other	23	5			12	6	
Farmer's Home Admin.	19	4		1		14	
Merchant	16	6				10	
Seed Company	14	3				11	
Chemical/Fertilizer Co.	13	9				4	
Swine Genetics Company	10	10					
Insurance Companies	10	8				2	
State/Local Government	4	1			1	2	
Small Business Administration	2				1	1	

Table 7.2 Initial filings by type of lender and subtype of producer
(NET = network, NFC = nonfamily corp.).

Lender type	Coop	Family	NET	NFC	NA
Banks		90	35	16	3
Machinery Dealer/Manufacturer	1	73	4	33	2
Swine Production Company		12	7		2
Farm Services Admin.		40	1		1
Farm Credit Services	28	21	3	4	2
Cooperative - Regional		12	6		7
Grain/ Feed Company		43	5		1
Individuals	2	6			1
Leasing Company	7	5	2	1	
Finance Company - Non Bank	1	4	1		
Cooperatives - Local		1			1
Uncertain/Other	2	3			
Farmer's Home Admin.		4			
Merchant		3			3
Seed Company		1		2	
Chemical/Fertilizer Co.	9				
Swine Genetics Company	4	2	3	1	
Insurance Companies		3	1	4	
State/Local Government		1			
Small Business Administration					

Table 7.3 Initial filings by type of lender and size of facilities.

Lender type	Total	1st	2nd	3rd	4th	NA
Banks	504	118	125	115	135	11
Machinery Dealer/Manufacturer	382	85	97	85	108	7
Swine Production Company	216	7	87	56	66	
Farm Services Admin.	212	71	55	58	27	1
Farm Credit Services	125	3	55	29	36	2
Cooperative - Regional	69	24	8	20	17	
Grain/ Feed Company	62	7	34	8	13	
Individuals	41	7	14	11	7	2
Leasing Company	33	7	17	4	5	
Finance Company - Non Bank	32	4	3	9	16	
Cooperatives - Local	26	14	3	2	7	
Uncertain/Other	23	13	4	2	4	
Farmer's Home Admin.	19	7	3	6	3	
Merchant	16	2	5	3	4	2
Seed Company	14	7	1	4	2	
Chemical/Fertilizer Co.	13	1	12			
Swine Genetics Company	10		4	1	5	
Insurance Companies	10	2	1		7	
State/Local Government	4	2	1	1		
Small Business Administration	2	1		1		

Table 7.4 Initial filings by asset size of bank and type of producer.

Quartile Assets	No. of filings	Corp.	LLC	Partners	Sole Prop.
1	59	21		3	35
2	87	19		3	65
3	122	31		4	87
4	176	48	3	10	115

Table 7.5 Initial filings by asset size of bank and subtype of producer.

Quartile Assets	No. of filings	Family	Network	Non family	NA
1	59	18	3		
2	87	13	2	4	
3	122	22	9		
4	176	34	12	4	1

Table 7.6 Initial filings by asset size of bank and quartile size of facilities.

Quartile Assets	No. of filings	1st	2nd	3rd	4th
1	59	29	12	9	8
2	87	19	18	23	27
3	122	19	43	27	29
4	176	37	40	43	50

Table 7.7 Initial filings by ag loan size of bank and type of producer.

Quartile Ag loans	No. of filings	Corp.	LLC	Partners	Sole Prop.
1	39	19		1	19
2	47	4		2	41
3	103	21		6	76
4	255	75	3	11	166

Table 7.8 Initial filings by ag loan size of bank and subtype of producer.

Quartile Ag loans	No. of filings	Family	Network	Non-family	NA
1	39	17	2		
2	47	3	1		
3	103	18	3		
4	255	49	20	8	1

Table 7.9 Initial filings by ag loan size of bank and quartile size of facilities.

Quartile Ag loans	No. of filings	1st	2nd	3rd	4th
1	39	21	8	4	5
2	47	15	11	16	5
3	103	16	34	27	26
4	255	52	60	55	78

Table 7.10 Filings by Murphy contractees to other lenders by producer type.

Lender type	Total	Corp.	Ptr.	Sole prop.	Trust
Swine Production Company	195	16	7	171	1
Banks	131	4	6	121	
Machinery Dealer/Manufacturer	77		4	73	
Farm Services Admin.	46	3		43	
Farm Credit Services	38	4		34	
Finance Company	17			17	
Farmer's Home Administration	8	1		7	
Individuals	7			7	
Leasing Company	5			5	
Seed Company	5			5	
Grain/Feed Company	5			5	
Merchant	5			5	
Chemical/Fertilizer	3			3	
Cooperatives - Local	3			3	
Uncertain/Other	2			2	
State/Local Government	1			1	
Cooperative - Regional	1			1	
Small Business Administration	1			1	

8 Extending the Models

The major theoretical issues discussed in the opening chapters of this book can now be addressed with the models of cooperation and competition developed above. The first issue concerns the types of explanations and models that can be developed by anthropologists studying economies and economic behavior. The second issue concerns the relationship between individual choice and institutional constraint in an economic system. The third issue concerns the practical problems of constructing social scientific knowledge in the American agricultural system where powerful players seek to shape knowledge creation to meet the interests of a few. Finally, the fourth issue concerns how the study of American agriculture can emerge from its recent preoccupations with classification to merge with the more holistic interests of an anthropology of institutions. In this chapter I explore the implications of my study on each of these issues.

Networks, Institutional Economics, and Social Structure

To recap the argument so far: recent technological developments have given rise to a spatially decentralized, component part system of industrial swine production. This industrialized production forms the basis for large-scale vertically integrated firms that pose a threat to the survival of small household producers. Land grant university advisers are urging farmers to duplicate these firms by forming their own cooperatively organized firms. The evidence suggests that the advice of the land grant experts may be misplaced. Their attempt to organize networks into large-scale firms may have the same outcome for networks as it did for the farmer cooperative movement - the creation of another class of vertically integrated firms ostensibly owned by farmers but benefiting hired management and private agribusiness. These recommendations seem to ignore the possibility that networks of household producers may organize outside of the market-firm continuum posited by institutional economics. A network itself may constitute a form of economic organization, distinct from though embedded in markets or firms, which emphasizes the nature of the relationships between parties (cf. Powell 1990, Powell and Smith-Doerr 1994 for a review of the network as economic entity; also see Plattner's 1984 concept of the equilibrating relationship). Not only is this network approach possibly a more viable strategy for small producers but it may very well explain the success of the industry's largest firm Murphy Farms.

It is the nature of the relationships between the actors in the networks described above that best explains the role of networks in the economy. Burt's concept of the 'structural hole' explains competition in markets and applies to the kind of networking arrangements occurring in Iowa's swine industry (Burt 1992). In Burt's terms the structural hole exists in the invisible gap between non-redundant contacts in a network. Advantage accrues to the player whose contacts are isolated from one another, that do not overlap. The entrepreneur is an entrepreneur by virtue of his or her occupancy of one of these holes in the social structure of information flows. In plain English this argument might be summed up as 'It's not what you know and it's not who you know. It's what you know about who you know that they don't know about each other.'

Such an explanation fits the case of Allan Garrison and many of the other organizers described above. It also describes the space occupied by Murphy Farms in a pattern of credit relationships. Network organizers and Murphy alike occupy a niche or hole in the sense that they know things about a large number of people who don't know these things about one another. The success of each has as much to do with their position in the flow of information as in the content of transactions. The real key is bringing the right information and opportunities to individuals who otherwise could not have obtained these resources. That is, in being in the position of linking contacts in ways not available to them as individuals.

Information is the key element to transaction costs. This suggests that it is the control over and the cost of information that explains the emergence of superior results in an economically competitive arena. Power, rather than being an abstract concept, is a technically definable advantage in the process of transacting which is held due to structural advantages in the flow of key information and attendant resources. It is connection rather than coercion that explains the successful player either at the micro level of the network or the macro level of the allocation of credit in an industry.

The existence of these patterns of interconnectedness argues against the folk ideology of the independent farmer. It also argues against various views of the inevitability of an economic process of consolidation of agricultural production under hierarchical forms of economic governance such as the mega-farm. Unlike the large firm, network producers can remain small scale and less capital intensive. Unlike the farm cooperative in which the farmer is marginalized as either a retail customer or the supplier of an undifferentiated commodity, the network organizes reciprocal relations between its members as component suppliers in an industrial process. Nevertheless, the prospect for a transformation of industrial swine production that benefits family farms is far from certain. There is, as Granovetter has noted, a 'high level of contingency' involved in network approaches to the sociology of economic life (Granovetter 1992). Still, a growing body of work has identified a number of industries where networking arrangements may constitute a valuable new form of economic governance alongside markets and firms (e.g. Dore 1983, Jarillo 1988, Larson 1992). Whatever the term used - relational contracting, equilibrating relationship, networks, or business groups - these forms may provide stable reciprocal relationships among participants in agro-industrial systems such as swine production just as they do for other industries where household production units and family based firms still predominate.

The explanation I've offered for the competitive success of the large-scale swine producers, particularly Murphy farms, is highly tentative. This model and the previous one, offered to explain the success of network organizers, constitute examples of abductive inference (on the origins of abductive reasoning see Josephson and Josephson 1996, for more on the role of abduction in economic explanation see Hodgson 1993).

Abductive inference is the kind of reasoning commonly used in daily life in a variety of tasks from negotiating traffic to medical diagnosis. An abductive inference claims to be 'probably' true inasmuch as it accounts for an event better than alternative explanations. Unlike the positivistic goals of deductive and inductive inference, abduction makes do with the evidence at hand, presenting a sort of 'causal story'. Abduction seems particularly suited to the goals of generalization in anthropology. Abductive inferences possess an emergent quality wherein the inference itself transcends the characteristics of the data. Analyzing each member of a network for characteristics that correlate with those of other members, whether in a small producer network or in a broad credit network, is not as useful in generating explanations as is interpreting the overall pattern. Abductive inference takes the individual units of observation and provides the causal story to describe their relationships. The explanation offered above for competitive success is an example of abductive inference that builds on the data in the previous chapters. It is, in effect, also a metaphorical explanation, extending the widely used term 'network' as both a social and visual metaphor to enhance our understanding of economic relationships.

The idea of a network as an explanatory tool for economics addresses two of the issues raised in chapter two (cf. Burt 1992 on networks and economic competitiveness). 'Networks' provide the basis for a broadly organic form of economic explanation in which both the behavior of individuals and the role of the institutions are united. The model of successful network organizing is also generative in the sense that it suggests or generates the model structure of relationships that is used to explain competitive success. The model of competitive success based on a network of relationships also follows Barth's claim that anthropological explanations should provide hypotheses about 'possible and impossible systems' rather than predictions.

Murphy Farms represents one possible variation in a system that uses a variety of institutions and rules to permit the creation of a dispersed yet integrated production network. Those institutions, involving financial, legal, and agricultural rules and practices, are endogenous to the decision making of farmers and corporations alike. Those institutions, as North noted, determine the available opportunities and organizations are created to take advantage of them. What remains to be seen is how the further evolution of these organizations will alter the institutions themselves.

The alteration of a society's institutional structure requires more than just the manipulation of a few economic players – it requires an alliance with all of those whose purview is the generation of knowledge about the society itself. Here Marx and Gramsci correctly identified the role of the educated classes in creating and shaping the ideology that justifies the economic interests of the state and the ruling class. It was against this knowledge building apparatus that Miner and Goldschmidt attempted to turn their observations of the changes taking place in American agriculture.

Goldschmidt identified the ways in which government policies and research priorities favored the control of agriculture by corporate interests. These interests have (Goldschmidt 1978:xxxii):

> repeatedly and effectively hidden behind the image of the farmer,
> the mythical downtrodden hayseed who is at once benighted and
> exploited and yet the 'backbone' of our country.

In much the same fashion my own work was often greeted with hostility since I was an outsider to the massive research and educational bureaucracy that supposedly 'serves' the farmer. The resistance encountered by researchers 50 years after Goldschmidt's original study is consistent with his analysis of the way in which powerful interests attempt to shape research priorities.

One of the most important observations to come out of this study of networking as an alternative farming strategy is the importance of information, of knowledge, and its use in empowering or oppressing citizens. The information networks that help to build a local cooperative or a Murphy Farms are by extension the same kind of networks that can build a resistance movement to an industrial process that threatens the health of an entire population. At the same time, if those who are charged with the basic responsibilities for the collection, analysis, and dissemination of information are stymied in that endeavor by special interests, the effective ability to protect the public good will be severely compromised. The cost of transacting, the cost of obtaining information, is too great for isolated groups and individuals to bear. The abandonment of the public trust that occurs when the state relinquishes its duty to inform as well as enforce challenges more fundamental institutions of a democratic society. It is this challenge to democratic freedoms that confronted Goldschmidt in the form of efforts to discredit his study. It is this same restriction of information to benefit the few that has led to similar challenges to the ability of many ordinary citizens to obtain information about the firms that operate in their communities.

One of the issues frequently brought out echoes Goldschmidt's comment above: what is a farmer? It is important to distinguish between farmers and corporations that hide behind the façade of the farmer. This illustrates a basic difference between the activities of those who would create knowledge and those who would create the rules of the economic game. In chapter 2 I criticized the taxonomic efforts of rural sociologists, yet I acknowledge the need to apply some definition of family farm to avoid the hypocrisy of the corporations hiding behind the claim to be farms. This is actually a consistent position: the role of knowledge creation should be to highlight the fluidity of classificatory schemes, to, in effect, bring to the attention of the rule makers the arbitrariness of their rules. In other words, it is not for social scientists to define farmers but to describe to policy makers the conditions of farming, its participants, organizations, and institutions, and their interrelationships, in such a way as to allow for open debate over whose interests the rules of the game will benefit. To do less, to pretend to define sharp categories where none exist, is to take the side of those who would manipulate the rules for their own benefit by claiming to be something they are not. Laws and policies create arbitrary definitions out of necessity. Social realities and economic life, as I've argued above, are products of human artifice, not of an impersonal 'nature'. The contribution of a holistic social science such as anthropology is to point out the institutional embeddedness of the construction of these definitions, to point out to all that the classifications employed are subject to debate and not a reflection of a fixed and immutable reality.

It's Not All Politics

Throughout this work I have tried to give equal emphasis to the choices of individuals and to the role of the institutions in which those choices are embedded. Anthropology is uniquely suited to this kind of dual perspective because of its commitment to the particularities of fieldwork combined with the generalizing goals of science. I realize that to take this position is to speak counter to the belief that institutions, particularly political institutions, can so enhance the power of certain groups as to render the decisions of the members of other groups meaningless. What I have reported here, from observations made in numerous church basements and coffee shops over two years of field research in Iowa, was a negotiated process of information gathering and decision making. I call it a negotiated process because the flow of information was never completely open or free as the neoclassical model would have it, nor was it totally constrained by the powerful as the more intransigent of Marxist models would have it. Instead what I saw ethnographically was a process through which individuals were tacking back and forth between what they knew, what they didn't know, and what they couldn't know. In establishing ties to one another some possessed clear advantages, advantages often conferred by social structure, often enhanced by aggressive pursuit of a goal. The networks of farms that have emerged to date have built on the ability of individuals to make choices, however limited, within the given system of economic and social institutions. The information structure of the economic system is extraordinarily porous, allowing participants to exchange information and construct relationships in many creative ways. That porosity is what gives rise to the new possibilities that can emerge from the existing system. The challenge facing anthropologists is to describe that system and its potential for variety, both for the sheer sense of 'watching and wondering' of which Barth spoke and for the power such observations have to aid in furthering that variety.

Bibliography

Acheson, James M. (1982), 'Limitations On Firm Size in a Tarascan Pueblo', *Human Organization,* 41:323-329.

Acheson, James M., (ed.) (1994), *Anthropology and Institutional Economics: Monographs in Economic Anthropology, No. 12,* Lanham, MD: University Press of America.

Adams, Jane (1994), *The Transformation of Rural Life: Southern Illinois, 1890-1990,* Chapel Hill, NC: The University of North Carolina Press.

———(1996), 'U.S. Farm Households and the Post-World War II Regime', Paper Presented at the 1996 Meeting of the Society for Economic Anthropology, Baltimore, MD.

Barkema, Alan and Michael L. Cook (1993), 'The Changing U.S. Pork Industry: A Dilemma for Public Policy', *Federal Reserve Bank of Kansas City Economic Review* Second Quarter 1993:49-65.

Barlett, Peggy (1989), 'Industrial Agriculture', in Plattner, Stuart, (ed.), *Economic Anthropology,* Stanford, CA: Stanford University Press.

———(1993), *American Dreams, Rural Realities: Family Farms in Crisis,* Chapel Hill: University of North Carolina Press.

Barlett, Peggy, (ed.), (1980), *Agricultural Decision Making,* New York: Academic Press.

Barnes, Donna A. and Audie Blevins (1992), 'Farm Structure and the Economic Well-Being of Nonmetropolitan Counties', *Rural Sociology,* 57(3):333-346.

———(1993), 'On Sinners and Saints: Reply to Gilles and Geletta and to Lobao, Schulman, and Swanson', *Rural Sociology,* 58(2):289-298.

Barnes, J.A. (1954), 'Class and Committees in a Norwegian Island Parish', *Human Relations,* 7:39-58.

Barth, Frederick (1981), *Process and From in Social Life: Selected Essays of Frederic Barth, Vol. 1,* London: Routledge and Kegan Paul.

Bates, Robert H. (1989), *Beyond the Miracle of the Market: The Political Economy of Agrarian Development in Kenya,* New York: Cambridge University Press.

———(1990), 'Macropolitical Economy in the Field of Development', in James Alt and Kenneth Shepsle, *Perspectives On Positive Political Economy,* New York: Cambridge University Press.

———(1995), 'Social Dilemmas and Rational Individuals: An Assessment of the New Institutionalism', in John Harriss, Janet Hunter, and Colin M. Lewis, *The New Institutional Economics and Third World Development,* New York: Routledge.

Beebe, James (1995), 'Basic Concepts and Techniques of Rapid Appraisal', *Human Organization,* 54(1):52-59.

Bennett, John (1968), 'Reciprocal Economic Exchanges Among North American Agricultural Operators', *Southwestern Journal of Anthropology*, 24:279-309.

——(1969), *Northern Plainsmen: Adaptive Strategy and Agrarian Life*, Arlington Heights, IL: AHM Publishing Corp.

——(1982), *Of Time and the Enterprise: North American Family Farm Management in a Context of Resource Marginality*, Minneapolis, MN: University of Minnesota Press.

Bhaskar, Roy (1979), *The Possibility of Naturalism: A Philosophical Critique of the Contemporary Human Sciences*, Atlantic Highlands, NJ: Humanities Press.

Boisevain, Jeremy (1974), *Friends of Friends: Networks, Manipulators, and Coalitions*, New York: St. Martin's Press.

Boissevain, Jeremy and J. Clyde Mitchell (1971), *Network Analysis: Studies in Human Interaction*, The Hague: Mouton.

Bott, Elizabeth (1971[1957]), *Family and Social Network: Roles, Norms, and External Relationships in Ordinary Urban Families*, London: Tavistock Publications.

Britan, Gerald M. (1987), 'The Politics of Agricultural Science', in *Farm Work and Field Work*, Michael Chibnik, (ed.) pp. 267-280, Ithaca, NY: Cornell University Press.

Bronstien, Barbara F. (1996), 'Booming Dutch Bank Cultivating Big Crop of U.S. Farm Loans, (Rabobank Nederland)', *American Banker*, Jan 29, 1996 V161 N18 P9(1).

Burt, Ronald (1992), *Structural Holes: The Social Structure of Competition*, Cambridge, MA: Harvard University Press.

Buttel, Frederick H. and Howard Newby (1980), *The Rural Sociology of the Advanced Societies: Critical Perspectives*, Montclair, NJ: Allanheld, Osmun Publishers.

Buttel, Frederick H., Olaf F. Larson, Gilbert W. Gillespie Jr. (1990), *The Sociology of Agriculture*, New York: Greenwood Press.

Campbell, John L., J. Rogers Hollingsworth, and Leon N. Lindberg (1991), *Governance of the American Economy*, Cambridge: Cambridge University Press.

Cancian, Frank (1966), 'Maximization As Norm, Strategy, and Theory: A Comment On Programmatic Statements in Economic Anthropology', *American Anthropologist*, 68:465-70.

——(1967), 'Stratification and Risk Taking: A Theory Tested On Agricultural Innovation', *American Sociological Review*, 32:912-927.

Chayanov, A. V. (1986[1966]) *The Theory of Peasant Economy*, Madison, WI: The University of Wisconsin Press.

Chibnik, Michael, (ed.) (1987), *Farm Work and Fieldwork: American Agriculture in Anthropological Perspective*, Ithaca, NY: Cornell University Press.

Coase, Ronald H. (1937), 'The Nature of the Firm', *Economica*, 4:386-405.

————(1960), 'The Problem of Social Cost', *Journal of Law and Economics,* 17, 53-71.

————(1993), 'The Nature of the Firm: Influence', in Williamson, Oliver and Sidney G. Winter, (eds.) *The Nature of the Firm: Origins, Evolution, and Development,* New York: Oxford University Press.

Cochrane, Willard (1993), *The Development of American Agriculture: A Historical Analysis,* Minneapolis, MN: University of Minnesota Press.

Collier, Andrew (1994), *Critical Realism: An Introduction to Roy Bhaskar's Philosophy,* London: Verso.

Cook, K. S. and J. M. Whitmeyer (1992), 'Two Approaches to Social Structure: Exchange Theory and Network Analysis', *Annual Review of Sociology,* 18:109-27.

Dalton, George (1969), 'Theoretical Issues in Economic Anthropology', *Current Anthropology,* 10(1):63-102.

Dalton, George, (ed.) (1967), *Tribal and Peasant Economies,* Austin, TX: University of Texas Press.

Davis, John Emmeus (1980), 'Capitalist Agricultural Development and the Exploitation of the Propertied Laborer', in Frederick Buttel and Howard Newby, (eds.) *The Rural Sociology of the Advanced Societies,* Montclair, NJ: Allanheld, Osmun.

Des Moines Register (1994), 'Letters to the Editor', May 29, 1994.

Donham, K. and K. Thu (1993), 'Relationships of Agricultural and Economic Policy to the Health of Farm Families, Livestock, and the Environment', *Journal of the American Veterinary Medical Association,* 202(7):1084-1091.

————(1995), 'Agricultural Medicine and Environmental Health: The Missing Component of the Sustainable Agricultural Movement', in *Human Sustainability in Agriculture,* H.H. McDuffie, *et al.,* (eds.) Boca Raton, Florida: Lewis Publishers.

Dore, Ronald (1980), 'Goodwill and the Spirit of Market Capitalism', *The British Journal of Sociology,* 34(4):459-482.

Dotson, Earl (ed.) (1994), *Networking: Competitive Positioning for Pork Producers,* Des Moines, IA: National Pork Producers Council.

1995), *Networking II: Competitive Positioning for Pork Producers,* Des Moines, IA: National Pork Producers Council.

Douglas, Mary (1992), 'Autonomy and Opportunism', in *Risk and Blame,* New York: Routledge.

Durkheim, Emile (1949[1893]), *The Division of Labor in Society,* George Simpson, Trans., Glencoe, IL: The Free Press.

————(1982[1896]), *The Rules of the Sociological Method,* Steven Lukes, (ed.) W.D. Halls, Trans. New York: The Free Press.

Durrenberger, E. Paul and Kendall M. Thu (1994), 'Our Changing Swine Industry and Signals of Discontent', *Iowa Groundwater Quarterly,* 5(4):5-7.

————(1996a) 'The Expansion of Large Scale Hog Farming in Iowa: The Applicability of Goldschmidt's Findings Fifty Years Later', *Human Organization,* 55(4).

————(1996b) 'The Industrialization of Swine Production in the U.S.: An Overview', *Culture & Agriculture,* 18(1):19-22.

Durrenberger, E. Paul, Kendall M. Thu, and Randy Ziegenhorn (1995), *Swine Producer Networks in Iowa, Project Report,* Leopold Center for Sustainable Agriculture, Iowa State University.

Easton, Geoffrey (1992), 'Industrial Networks: A Review', in Bjorn Axelsson and Geoffrey Easton, (eds.), *Industrial Networks: A New View of Reality,* New York: Routledge.

Eggertsson, Thrainn (1990), *Economic Behavior and Institutions,* New York: Cambridge University Press.

Ensminger, Jean (1992), *Making a Market: The Institutional Transformation of an African Society,* New York, NY: Cambridge University Press.

Firth, Raymond (1939), *Primitive Polynesian Economy,* London: George Routledge and Sons.

Freeman, Linda K. (1988), 'The Co-Op Strategy', *Food Engineering,* 60:68-9.

Friedland, William H. (1982), 'The End of Rural Society and the Future of Rural Sociology', *Rural Sociology,* 47(4):589-608.

Friedman, Milton (1953), 'The Methodology of Positive Economics', in Friedman, Milton, *Essays in Positive Economics,* Chicago: The University of Chicago Press.

Friedmann, Harriet (1978a), 'World Market, State, and Family Farm: Social Bases of Household Production in the Era of Wage Labor', *Comparative Studies in Society and History,* 20:545-586.

————(1978b), 'Simple Commodity Production and Wage Labor in the American Plains', *The Journal of Peasant Studies,* 6(1):71-99.

————(1980), 'Household Production and the National Economy: Concepts for The Analysis of Agrarian Formations', *Journal of Peasant Studies,* 7(2):158-184.

————(1988), 'Form and Substance in the Analysis of the World Economy', in Wellman, Berry and S.D. Berkowitz 1988, *Social Structures: A Network Approach,* Cambridge: Cambridge University Press.

Friedmann, Harriet and Phillip McMichael (1989), 'Agriculture and the State System', *Sociologia Ruralis,* 29(2):93-117.

Geertz, Clifford (1992[1978]), 'The Bazaar Economy: Information and Search in Peasant Marketing', in Granovetter, Marc and Richard Swedberg, *The Sociology of Economic Life,* Boulder, CO: Westview Press.

Gilbert, Jess and Raymond Akor (1988), 'Increasing Structural Divergence in U.S. Dairying: California and Wisconsin Since 1950', *Rural Sociology,* 53(1):56-72.

Gilles, Jere and Simon Geletta (1993), 'Farm Structure and Economic Well-Being: A Look at Three Methodological Sins', *Rural Sociology*, 58(2):269-276.

Gilles, Jere Lee and Michael Dalecki (1988), 'Rural Well Being and Agricultural Change in Two Farming Regions', *Rural Sociology*, 53(1):40-55.

Gladwin, Christina and Kathleen Truman, (eds.) (1989), *Food and Farm*, Lanham, MD: University of America Press.

Godelier, Maurice (1972), *Rationality and Irrationality in Economics*, New York: Monthly Review Press.

———(1984), *The Mental and the Material*, London: Verso.

Goldschmidt, Walter (1978[1949]), *As You Sow: Three Studies in the Social Consequences of Agribusiness*, Montclair, NJ: Allanheld, Osmun and Co.

Goodfellow, D. M. (1939), *Principles of Economic Sociology*, Philadelphia, PA: P. Blakiston's Son & Co., Inc.

Goodman, David, Bernardo Sorj, and John Wilkinson (1987), *From Farming to Biotechnology: A Theory of Agro-Industrial Development*, Oxford: Basil Blackwell.

Granovetter, Mark (1985), 'Economic Action, Social Structure, and Embeddedness', *American Journal of Sociology*, 91:481-510.

———(1992), 'The Nature of Economic Relations', in Sutti Ortiz and Susan Lees, (eds.) *Understanding Economic Process*, Lanham, MD: University Press of America.

Green, Gary P. (1985), 'Large-Scale Farming and the Quality of Life in Rural Communities: Further Specification of the Goldschmidt Hypothesis', *Rural Sociology*, 50(2):262-274.

Harl, Neil E. (1990), *The Farm Debt Crisis of the 1980s*, Ames, IA: Iowa State University Press.

Harris, Craig K. and Jess Gilbert (1982), 'Large-Scale Farming, Rural Income, and Goldschmidt's Agrarian Thesis', *Rural Sociology*, 47(3):449-458.

Harris, Marvin (1968), *The Rise of Anthropological Theory*, New York: Harper and Row.

Heffernan, William D, (1972), 'Sociological Dimensions of Agricultural Structures in the United States', *Sociologia Ruralis*, 12(3/4):481-99.

Heffernan, William D. and Paul Lasley (1978), 'Agricultural Structure and Interaction in the Local Community: A Case Study', *Rural Sociology*, 43(3):348-361.

Herskovits, Melville (1952), *Economic Anthropology*, New York: Alfred A. Knopf.

Hightower, Jim (1978[1972]), *Hard Tomatoes, Hard Times*, Cambridge, MA: Schenkman Publishing Co.

Hodgson, Geoffrey M. (1996), *Economics and Evolution: Bringing Life Back Into Economics*, Ann Arbor, Michigan: University of Michigan Press.

Ingold, Tim (1996), 'Introduction', in Tim Ingold, (ed.), *Key Debates in Anthropology*, New York: Routledge.

Iowa Agricultural Statistics (1996), *Iowa Operations With Hogs*, Miscellaneous Publications, Des Moines, IA: Iowa Department of Agriculture and Land Stewardship.

Jarillo, J. Carlos (1988), 'On Strategic Networks', *Strategic Management Journal*, 9:31-41.

Jereski, Laura and Randall Smith (1996), 'Morgan Stanley's Pig-Farm Dream Wallows in Losses, Spatters Clients', *Wall Street Journal*, May 26, 1996.

Josephson, John R. and Susan G. Josephson, (eds.) (1996), *Abductive Inference: Computation, Philosophy, and Technology*, Cambridge: Cambridge University Press.

Knight, Frank (1921), *Risk, Uncertainty and Profit*, Boston: Houghton Mifflin.

Kravitz, Linda (1974), *Who's Minding the Co-Op? A Report On Farmer Control of Farmer Cooperatives*, Washington, DC: Agribusiness Accountability Project.

Landa, Janet Tai (1994), *Trust, Ethnicity, and Identity: Beyond the New Institutional Economics of Ethnic Trading Networks, Contract Law and Gift Exchange*, Ann Arbor: University of Michigan Press.

Larson, Andrea (1992), 'Network Dyads in Entrepreneurial Settings: A Study of the Governance of Exchange Relationships', *Administrative Science Quarterly*, 37:76-104.

Lawrence, John (1995), 'Ten Year Summary of Estimated Hog Returns', in *ISU Swine Research Report*, Ames, Iowa: Iowa State University.

Leclair, Edward, and Harold Schneider, (eds.) (1968), *Economic Anthropology: Readings in Theory and Analysis*, New York: Holt, Rinehart and Winston, Inc.

Lee, Louise (1996), 'Weak Poultry Sales Hurt Small Growers', *The Wall Street Journal*, June 12, 1996 B1.

Levi-Strauss, Claude (1963), *Structural Anthropology*, New York: Basic Books.

———(1966), *The Savage Mind*, Chicago: University of Chicago Press.

Little, Peter D. and Michael J. Watts, (eds.) (1994), *Living Under Contract: Contract Farming and Agrarian Transformation in Sub-Saharan Africa*, Madison, WI: The University of Wisconsin Press.

Lobao, Linda M. and Michael D. Schulman (1991), 'Farming Pattern, Rural Restructuring, and Poverty: A Comparative Regional Analysis', *Rural Sociology*, 56(4):565-602.

Lobao, Linda M. and Michael D. Schulman and Louis E. Swanson (1993), 'Still Going: Recent Debates On the Goldschmidt Hypothesis', *Rural Sociology*, 58(2):277-288.

Lobao-Reif, Linda (1987), 'Farm Structure, Industry Structure, and Socioeconomic Conditions in the United States', *Rural Sociology*, 52(4):462-482.

Macaulay, Stewart (1963), 'Non-Contractual Relations in Business: A Preliminary Study', *American Sociological Review*, 28:55-67.

Malinowski, Bronislaw (1984[1922]) *Argonauts of the Western Pacific*, Prospect Heights, IL: Waveland Press, Inc.

Mann, Susan A. and James M. Dickinson (1978), 'Obstacles to the Development of Capitalist Agriculture', *Journal of Peasant Studies*, 5(4):466-81.

———(1987), 'One Furrow Forward, Two Furrows Back: A Marx-Weber Synthesis for Rural Sociology', *Rural Sociology*, 52(2):264-285.

Marcus, George E. and Michael M. J. Fisher (1986), *Anthropology As Cultural Critique: An Experimental Moment in the Human Sciences*, Chicago: University of Chicago Press.

Marsden, Terry, Richard Munton, Sarah Whatmore and Jo Little (1986), 'Towards a Political Economy of Capitalist Agriculture: A British Perspective', *International Journal of Urban and Regional Research*, 4:498-521.

Marx, Karl (1965[1906]) *Capital, A Critique of Political Economy*, (ed.) F Engels, New York: Random House.

Mauss, Marcel (1990[1925]) *The Gift, Forms and Functions of Exchange in Archaic Societies*, New York: W. W. Norton.

Miner, Horace (1949), *Culture and Agriculture: An Anthropological Study of a Corn-Belt County*, University of Michigan Press.

Mitchell, J. Clyde (1974), 'Social Networks', in Siegel, Bernard J. *et al.* (eds.) *Annual Review of Anthropology*, Palo Alto, CA: Annual Reviews, Inc.

Mooney, Patrick H. (1982), 'Labor Time, Production Time and Capitalist Development in Agriculture: A Reconsideration of the Mann-Dickinson Thesis', *Sociologia Ruralis*, 22(3/4):279-292.

———(1983), 'Toward a Class Analysis of Midwestern Agriculture', *Rural Sociology*, 48(4):563-584.

———(1986), 'The Political Economy of Credit in American Agriculture', *Rural Sociology*, 51(4):449-470.

———(1987), 'Desperately Seeking: One-Dimensional Mann and Dickinson', *Rural Sociology*, 52(2):286-295.

Newby, Howard (1978), 'The Rural Sociology of Advanced Capitalist Societies', in Newby, Howard, (ed.) *International Perspectives in Rural Sociology*, New York: John Wiley and Sons.

North, Douglas (1977), 'Markets and Other Allocation Systems in History: The Challenge of Karl Polanyi', *Journal of European Economic History*, 6:703-716.

———(1981), *Structure and Change in Economic History*, New York: W.W. Norton.

———(1986), 'Is It Worth Making Sense of Marx?', *Inquiry*, 29:57-63.

———(1990), *Institutions, Institutional Change and Economic Performance*, New York: Cambridge University Press.

Nuckton, Carole Frank, Refugio I. Rochin and Douglas Gwynn (1982), 'Farm Size and Rural Community Welfare: An Interdisciplinary Approach', *Rural Sociology* 47(1):32-46.

Ortner, Sherry (1984), 'Theory in Anthropology Since The Sixties', *Comparative Studies of Society and History*, 26:126-66.

Outhwaite, William (1987), *New Philosophies of Science: Realism, Hermeneutics and Critical Theory*, New York: St. Martin's Press.

Palsson, Gisli and Durrenberger, E. Paul (1993), 'Icelandic Foremen and Skippers: The Structure and Evolution of a Folk Model', *American Ethnologist*, 10(3):511-528.

Paulsen, Arnold and Michael Rahm (1979), *Development of Subsidiary Sow-Farrowing Firms in Iowa*, Ames, IA: Agriculture and Home Economics Experiment Station.

Perkins, Jerry (1995), 'Foreign Capital Sought for Hog Farm', Des Moines, Iowa: *Des Moines* Register, February 18.

Plattner, Stuart (1984), 'Equilibrating Market Relationships' In Stuart Plattner, (ed.), *Markets and Marketing*, Lanham, MD: University Press of America.

———(1989a) 'Introduction', in Stuart Plattner, (ed.), *Economic Anthropology*, Stanford, CA: Stanford University Press.

———(1989b) 'Economic Behavior in Markets', in Stuart Plattner (ed.), *Economic Anthropology*, Stanford, CA: Stanford University Press.

Polanyi, Karl (1944), *The Great Transformation*, New York: Farrar & Rinehart, Inc.

———(1957), 'The Economy As Instituted Process', in Karl Polanyi, Conrad M. Arensberg, and Harry W. Pearson, (eds.) *Trade and Market in Early Empires*, Glencoe, IL: The Free Press.

Porter, Michael E. (1990), *The Competitive Advantage of Nations*, New York: The Free Press.

Portz, John (1991), 'Economic Governance and the American Meatpacking Industry', in John L. Campbell, J. Rogers Hollingsworth, and Leon N. Lindberg *Governance of the American Economy*, Cambridge: Cambridge University Press.

Posner, Richard A. (1980), 'A Theory of Primitive Society With Special Reference to Law', *Journal of Law and Economics*, 23:1-53.

Powell, Walter W. (1990), 'Neither Market Nor Hierarchy: Network Forms of Organization', *Research in Organizational Behavior*, 12:295-336.

Powell, Walter W. and Laural Smith-Doerr (1994), 'Networks and Economic Life', in Neil J. Smelser and Richard Swedburg (eds.), *The Handbook of Economic Sociology*, Princeton, N.J.: Princeton University Press.

Prior, Jean C. (1991), *Landforms of Iowa*, Iowa City, IA: University of Iowa Press.

Radcliffe-Brown, A.R. (1952), *Structure and Function in Primitive Society*, New York: The Free Press.

Rasmussen, Wayne D. (1991), *Farmers, Cooperatives, and USDA: A History of Agricultural Cooperative Service*, Washington, DC: USDA.

Rawski, Thomas G. *et al.* (eds.) (1996), *Economics and the Historian*, Berkeley: University of California Press.

Rehfus, Melissa and Christina Gladwin (1994), 'Individual Choice and Institutional Constraints: The New Organization of Health Care in the USA', in Acheson, James, (ed.) 1994, *Anthropology and Institutional Economics*, Lanham, MD: University Press of America.

Riker, William H. (1990), 'Political Science and Rational Choice', in James Alt and Kenneth Shepsle, *Perspectives On Positive Political Economy*, New York: Cambridge University Press.

Rodefeld, Richard (1974), *The Changing Organizational and Occupational Structure of Farming and the Implications for Farm Workforce Individuals, Families, and Communities*, Unpublished Ph.D. Dissertation, University of Wisconsin.

Ryan, Bryce and Neal C. Gross (1943), 'The Diffusion of Hybrid Seed Corn in Two Iowa Communities', *Rural Sociology*, 8:15-24.

Sahlins, Marshall (1972), *Stone Age Economics*, Chicago: Aldine Atherton Inc.

Samuelson, Paul A. and William D. Nordhaus (1992), *Economics*, 14th Edition, New York: McGraw-Hill.

Schneider, Harold K. (1974), *Economic Man*, New York: Macmillan Publishing Co.

Scott, James C. (1976), *The Moral Economy of the Peasant*, New Haven, CT: Yale University Press.

Sheshunoff Information Services (1996), *Banks of Iowa*, Austin, Texas: Sheshunoff Information Services.

Shipton, Parker (1994), 'Time and Money in the Western Sahel: A Clash of Cultures in Gambian Rural Finance', in Acheson, James, (ed.) 1994, *Anthropology and Institutional Economics*, Lanham, MD: University Press of America.

Smelser, Neil J. and Richard Swedburg (1994), 'The Sociological Perspective On the Economy', in Smelser, Neil J. and Richard Swedburg, *The Handbook of Economic Sociology*, Princeton, NJ: Princeton University Press.

Spiro, Melford (1992), 'Anthropological Other Or Burmese Brother?' *Studies in Cultural Analysis*, New Brunswick, NJ: Transaction Publishers.

Stinchcombe, Arthur L. (1986[1961]), 'Agricultural Enterprise and Rural Class Relations', in Arthur Stinchcombe, *Stratification and Organization*, Cambridge: Cambridge University Press.

Stull, Donald D., Michael J. Broadway, and David Griffith, (eds.) (1995), *Any Way You Cut It: Meat Processing in Small-Town America*, Lawrence, KS: University of Kansas Press.

Team Pork (1994), *Community Nursery Handbook*, Ames, Iowa: Iowa State University Extension.

Thu, K. (1996a) 'Piggeries and Politics: Rural Development and Iowa's Multibillion Dollar Swine Industry', *Culture & Agriculture*, 53:19-23.

———(1996b) *Understanding the Impacts of Large-Scale Swine Production: Proceedings From an Interdisciplinary Scientific Workshop*, Editor, Iowa City, Iowa: The University of Iowa.

Thu, K. and E. P. Durrenberger (1994), 'North Carolina's Hog Industry: The Rest of the Story', *Culture and Agriculture*, 49:20-23.

———(1995), 'The Subjective Versus Objective Myth: Verbal Reports and Physical Data in Swine Odor Research', *Proceedings of the International Livestock Odor Conference '95*, Ames, Iowa: Iowa State University.

———(1997), 'Selling the Farm and Makin' Bacon: Land Grant Institutions and Factory Hog Production', Paper Presented at the 1997 Meeting of the Society for Applied Anthropology, Seattle, WA.

Thu, K., K. Donham, R. Ziegenhorn, S. Reynolds, P.S. Thorne, P. Subramanian, P. Whitten, and J. Stookesberry (1997), 'A Control Study of the Physical and Mental Health of Residents Living Near a Large Scale Swine Operation', *Journal of Agricultural Safety and Health*, 3(1).

Thurnwald, Richard (1965[1932]), *Economics in Primitive Communities*, Oxford: Oxford University Press.

Toye, John (1995), 'The New Institutional Economics and Its Implications for Development Theory', in John Harriss, Janet Hunter, and Colin M. Lewis, *The New Institutional Economics and Third World Development*, New York: Routledge.

Vail, David J. (1982), 'Family Farms in the Web of Community: Exploring the Rural Political Economy of the United States', *Antipode*, 14(3):26-38.

Wellman, Berry and S. D. Berkowitz (1988), *Social Structures: A Network Approach*, Cambridge: Cambridge University Press.

White, Harrison C. (1988), 'Varieties of Markets', in Wellman, Berry and S. D. Berkowitz (1988), *Social Structures: A Network Approach*, Cambridge: Cambridge University Press.

Whitten, Norman E. and Alvin W. Wolfe (1973), 'Network Analysis', in Honigmann, John, (ed.) *Handbook of Social and Cultural Anthropology*, Chicago: Rand McNally.

Williamson, Oliver (1975), *Markets and Hierarchies: Analysis and Antitrust Implications*, New York: The Free Press.

———(1985), *The Economic Institutions of Capitalism: Firms, Markets, Relational Contracting*, New York: The Free Press.

Williamson, Oliver and Sidney G. Winter, (eds.) (1993), *The Nature of the Firm: Origins, Evolution, and Development*, New York: Oxford University Press.

Wrong, Dennis (1961), 'The Oversocialized Conception of Man in Modern Sociology', *American Sociological Review*, 26:183-96.

Young, Brigitte (1991), 'The Dairy Industry: From Yeomanry to the Institutionalization of Multilateral Governance', in Campbell, John L., J. Rogers Hollingsworth, and Leon N. Lindberg 1991 *Governance of the American Economy*, Cambridge: Cambridge University Press.

Ziegenhorn, Randy (1996), 'Get Together and Stay in: Swine Producer Networks in Iowa', Paper Presented at the 1996 Meeting of the Society for Economic Anthropology, Bethlehem, PA.

Index

For Product Safety Concerns and Information please contact our EU
representative GPSR@taylorandfrancis.com Taylor & Francis Verlag GmbH,
Kaufingerstraße 24, 80331 München, Germany

Printed and bound by CPI Group (UK) Ltd, Croydon, CR0 4YY
08/05/2025
01864411-0002